HACKING

THE

HACKING
THE
SAT

**Tips & Tricks to
Help You Prepare, Plan Ahead,
and Increase Your Score**

NEIL KHAUND | JASON BREITKOPF

Skyhorse Publishing

Skyhorse Publishing books may be purchased in bulk at special discounts for sales promotion, corporate gifts, fund-raising, or educational purposes. Special editions can also be created to specifications. For details, contact the Special Sales Department, Skyhorse Publishing, 307 West 36th Street, 11th Floor, New York, NY 10018 or info@skyhorsepublishing.com.

Skyhorse® and Skyhorse Publishing® are registered trademarks of Skyhorse Publishing, Inc.®, a Delaware corporation.

Visit our website at www.skyhorsepublishing.com.

10 9 8 7 6 5 4 3 2 1

Library of Congress Cataloging-in-Publication Data is available on file.

Cover design by Peter Donahue

Print ISBN: 978-1-63158-509-8
Ebook ISBN: 978-1-63158-510-4

Printed in the United States of America

CONTENTS

CONTENTS

Introduction
THE VALUE OF
THE PROCESS

After working with over fifty thousand students from around the country across thirty-five years there is one strategy that works every single time for increasing your SAT and ACT scores. If you put the work in, you get results. There is no substitute for hard work on these exams. Now, this book will provide you with some tips and guidelines to maximize your effort, but there is simply no shortcut to these exams. They are difficult and they require effort, but in the end they are manageable. Millions of students have survived the process and you will, too, but you first need to get in the mindset that you will need to hustle. There's no way around it.

That said we have seen many students who understand this fact but take it to the extreme like their lives depend on it. While these exams are important it's essential to have some perspective that this is only one step in a long and exciting academic journey. We coach students as much as possible that the process of test preparation is just as important as the result.

If you think about it, up until now in most students' high school careers there haven't been exams as critical towards determining their future as the college entrance exams are. There is quite a bit of pressure to score well on these exams as they not only help determine where you go to college but the types of scholarships and grants you could potentially qualify for. However, keep in mind that over your academic career this will not be the last high-stakes exam you will take. There could be others along your journey from master's exams such as the GRE, GMAT, MCAT, or LSAT to industry certifications you may need for your career like passing the bar or your Series 7.

The point is that if the SAT or the ACT is your first high-stakes exam take this opportunity to have some perspective on the process and remember that you are building a mindset to cope with these high-stakes academic endeavors. Regardless of the outcome, if you take the time and effort to prep for these exams you can be confident that you are going into them sitting in a better position than if you didn't take these exams seriously. While this may sound obvious it's important to know that you have the capacity to work extremely hard towards a goal and, regardless of the final score, know that you gave it a real shot. This level of mental acuity is critical in not only building confidence towards the exams but having the relaxed mindset necessary during the exam that you have already succeeded by maximizing the process.

The reason this perspective is so important is that there is no strategy, program, tutor, or curriculum that can help you get a better score without the extraordinary amount of effort required on your part. Frankly, there is no reason to read this book or any others if you don't go into the process with the mindset of "I am ready to work."

This book will help lift the veil on the test prep industry in order to give each consumer the knowledge they need to maximize their SAT or

ACT preparation process. While our strategies are among the best, and you will get a chance to learn them in detail, it's also important that each student understand how to maximize the process from knowing when to take the exam, which exam to take, and a buyer's guide on how to shop for a preparation program. Ultimately, this information can only be useful as part of a focused effort towards these exams.

Good luck and get to work!

Chapter 1
HOW TO USE THIS BOOK

I have worked in the supplemental education field for most of my adult life. And by supplemental education, I mean after-school and weekend tutoring. In that time, the majority of my clients and their children, the actual students, have hailed from backgrounds on the high end of the socio-economic scale. This is because tutoring is expensive.

I lived in the Los Angeles metro area for ten years, and, for the most part, made my living either as an in-home tutor or by working in, and managing, tutoring businesses. In my experience as an in-home tutor, I would drive from my small apartment near downtown Burbank, California, a decidedly low–middle- and working-class neighborhood, to places with recognizable names such as Beverly Hills, Bel-Air, Sherman Oaks, and Woodland Hills.

What I encountered was unimaginable wealth. My clients owned enormous homes, multiple expensive cars, and all the best life had to offer. They sent their children, my students, to the most prestigious private schools on the West Coast. And they could easily afford to pay the fees for in-home tutoring. In my time working with these students, I taught test preparation programs for the SAT, ACT, SAT Subject Tests, and Advanced Placement (AP) tests, as well as programs in test preparation for the SSAT and ISEE, private high school admittance tests, study skills, writing, various math subjects, and other academic topics.

The companies for which I worked would often develop programs for school partners, many of which were in disadvantaged neighborhoods. These programs brought my services and the programs I taught to students who would normally not be able to afford test prep and academic programs enjoyed by the wealthiest of families. Thanks to public school districts or large and well-known nonprofit organizations who partnered with my employers, I and my fellow tutors were able to provide the same curricula, materials, and instruction to students seeking to lift themselves up out of difficult economic situations and reach for academic success at college and beyond.

Invariably, though, whether the students with whom I worked were disadvantaged students from depressed socio-economic conditions or the children of wealth, these students all had one factor in common. Someone was paying a large amount of money for these programs. Wealthy parents paid the tutoring company directly for one-on-one attention from a tutor, often in their homes, while middle income families accessed these programs through modestly priced small-group classes and workshops at suburban tutoring centers. Lower income families accessed these same programs through their school district or a large, prestigious nonprofit organization in larger workshops and bootcamps. Whether I was working in the Los Angeles, New York, or Boston metropolitan areas, in the big city or in the close suburbs, there was a network of school districts, communities, and organizations in place to help students access the high-quality, expensive tutoring programs I taught.

Unfortunately, not every student has this opportunity. Perhaps your family resides in a rural community. Perhaps you participate in a homeschooling program. Perhaps your family lives in an urban environment without access to the resources that would connect students to test prep or tutoring programs. Only a small percentage of high school students in the United States can access high-quality test prep programs due to either cost or convenience, and often both.

While more and more high schools have begun to offer homegrown test prep programs, these programs often fail to result in any significant improvement in test scores. The reason for this failure can be surprising. When the staff at a typical high school develops a test prep program for the SAT or ACT, they often focus the instruction on the content of the test, meaning reviews of math concepts, grammar drills, and extra high school English classes. The mistake being made is that the SAT and the ACT are standardized tests covering topics that most high school juniors should have long mastered. These homegrown programs ignore the structure and format of the tests and misunderstand why the tests are structured the way they are structured.

In this book, we hope to provide a beacon of hope to educators, guidance and college counselors, school administrators, parents, and students. In these pages, you will find step by step instructions on how to build your own successful SAT or ACT program. Based on our years of experience doing this both in our tutoring centers and for our school and nonprofit partners, you can create a program that meets the needs of the students, provides an actionable plan for score improvement, and places results in the proper context for college application success.

This book will be organized in two distinct fashions. First, we will lay out the process for creating and completing a full SAT or ACT test prep program. This will include discussions of the tools and materials available, the environments in which programs work best, best practices for structuring a successful program, and how to supplement instruction with homework and practice tests. The best way to achieve your goals is to have a clear and organized plan.

Second, we will address the concerns of the different stakeholders in the test preparation process. How you use this book may very well depend on who you are in the test prep and college application process. If you are a parent, your questions and concerns will often be quite different than if you are the superintendent of a small, rural school district. If you are a student, your resources are probably quite different from those of an administrator at a community center. If you are a guidance counselor at an under-resourced public high school in a small, urban environment, your needs are often very different than if you run a home-school co-op.

Despite the fact that the SAT and the ACT are standardized tests, the program that best suits the needs of students studying to improve their results on these tests is a highly personalized and individualized experience. Every single SAT or ACT program I have taught has gone "off script" at one point, or more likely at several points. Beyond the academic reasons that I have had to adjust my teaching style and techniques, each individual with whom I have worked has had a different background; different family dynamic; different goals; and different social, emotional, and academic needs.

The SAT or ACT program you hack into being will be unique to you and your circumstances—and that is a good thing. The point is to build it to your needs and goals. In addition to a discussion on how to set realistic goals based on academic performance and previous scores, we will also look at how different circumstances and resources can lead to programs that look different from each other but can be equally successful.

Think of this book as the blueprint for designing your own SAT or ACT program. Each person who reads this book and uses the information to build a program will have different resources available. To push this analogy further, you might build the countertops in the kitchen from marble or you can use granite. Some may only have laminate available, but in the end, you will have the countertops you need to get the job done.

STUDENTS

If you are a high school student reading this book in order to build your own personal SAT or ACT program, congratulations on being one of the most self-motivated students I will have ever encountered. One of the reasons why test prep tutoring and classes work so effectively is that the vast majority of students are not self-motivated enough to log on to Khan Academy to practice for the SAT, for example, without external motivation. This is not a criticism of high school students. The biggest flaw with online learning is that it is counterintuitive to how humans learn.

Humans are pack animals. Generally, we learn best by working together. This is why group instruction, from preschool through graduate school and beyond to corporate trainings and the like, is still the most common method for instruction and for learning. In group settings, not only do students learn from the instructor, students learn from each other.

Tutoring works because students have access to support and expertise provided by a real, live person. While not always as effective as in-person tutoring, live tutoring over the internet is still generally more effective than video and text based lessons, because there is a person who can respond to the needs of the student, especially when the student has a question that may seem tangential to the immediate topic.

Colleges that offer online courses do not merely post the readings and assignments on the internet. Invariably, the courses are centered around either live or recorded lectures by professors. Merely seeing the face and hearing the voice of the professor explaining the topic results in a vast improvement in engagement and student performance.

Not all students have either the opportunity to take or the wherewithal to afford a test prep course, either in person or online. Whether you live in an isolated rural area or have severe financial constraints, you can use the blueprint provided by this book to build your own SAT or ACT program to meet your specific needs. While you are better served by working with an educator, whether a teacher from school, a tutor, or a concerned parent, you can build and complete a program on your own. It requires self-discipline.

The most important step for students in this process is the first step. Setting realistic, achievable goals can set you on the path for success. This includes not only setting goals for your test scores, but goals for the colleges and universities to which you plan to apply. Students have a tendency to either shoot too high or too low when building their college list. This is often because students only choose schools for their list based on having heard of those schools through casual conversation and popular culture. Many students have heard of the most prestigious colleges and universities, like the Ivy League schools, because they are often featured as locations in movies, television shows, and novels, and students are often aware of the local community colleges and noncompetitive four-year schools from peers who have attended these institutions or have selected them as safety schools.

Most people don't realize that there are over four thousand colleges and universities in the United States alone, and almost everyone can find a school that is a good match for their academic and social needs. Even though it doesn't seem like this is a part of the test preparation process, building an appropriate college list is integral to success in test prep. You don't know how far you need to go unless you set a goal.

PARENTS

It is more difficult than ever for parents to help their children with academics. Factors far outside the control of any one individual have caused massive changes in education and the college application process. Changes in education theory have led teachers to adjust their methods for explaining concepts in class. The most obvious example of this is the myth of "new" math. While math has not changed, some of the methods teachers use to explain the concepts have changed. The frustration parents feel when they can no longer help their children with homework has become such a cultural touchstone that popular films such as *The Incredibles 2* as well as other films and television shows have utilized this frustration for comedic effect.

The college application process is more complicated as well. More students than ever are applying for admission to colleges in the United States. Additionally, individual students are applying to more colleges on average than students did even ten or twenty years ago. Due to the increase in applications from both these factors, colleges are more and more selective than ever.

As late as the 1980s, only approximately 30 percent of high school students attended college at all. Due to policy changes enacted by the

Clinton administration beginning in 1993, that percentage has risen to over 70 percent of high school students who eventually attend some form of college.

The average number of colleges to which students apply has also steadily risen. Based on the information available from the 1970s through the 1990s, most students applied to anywhere from three to five colleges on average. They did so by filling out paper applications by hand or by carefully typing their responses onto applications. The average number of schools to which students apply today has risen from seven just a decade ago to ten according to a 2018 survey by researchers at the National Association for College Admission Counseling (NACAC). News reports of students who have applied to over twenty colleges and universities have become more common as well.

One of the most selective universities in the country, Harvard, is a perfect example of the result of these increases in applications. In the late 1980s, Harvard saw an average of 5,000 students apply each year for approximately 1,000 freshman seats. In 2017, Harvard saw approximately 40,000 students apply for 2,000 freshman seats. Despite doubling the number of students accepted and matriculating into Harvard, the acceptance rate has plunged from 20 percent to 5 percent over the last thirty years.

Parents are understandably concerned about what they can do to maximize their children's chances to attend the college of their choice. Increasing hard numbers like grade point averages and test scores is one way to do so. Tutoring for the SAT and ACT has grown by leaps and bounds over the last thirty years.

Unfortunately, not all parents have access to a reputable tutoring center and even when the local high school offers test prep, the program is not always as useful and successful as it could be.

Whether on their own or by joining together at a local community center, parents can put together a successful test prep program using the suggestions and tips in this book. Parents will find information on what space will work best for a test prep class, how to organize a syllabus, and what materials will provide the most effective learning experiences.

Despite the potential lack of professional tutoring services available to parents, either due to location or finances, finding a partner, such as a nonprofit organization like the Boys & Girls Club or the Girl Scouts, a fraternal organization like Rotary or the Lions Club, or your local school district or community college, can be invaluable, if only for the types of spaces they can provide.

The most important thing to remember is that you are not alone. Working together with other parents will result in a more successful experience for students. Pooling resources and partnering with each other can reduce costs for each individual and provide stability and regularity to a test prep course, which can ensure a higher degree of success.

EDUCATORS AND ADMINISTRATORS

We live in a time when communities have reduced school budgets to the bare minimum and beyond. Schools across the country struggle to assemble a complete staff, and programs in the arts and sciences are cut mercilessly. Guidance and college counseling programs have been reduced to a shadow of their former selves. This has resulted in an understandable decimation of services.

This is not a critique of school administrators, faculty, or staff. There are forces at play far beyond the control of individual high school principals and teachers. What has happened over the last thirty to fifty years is a systemic problem that has laid greater and greater pressure and responsibility on local administrators and teaching staffs.

The result is that guidance or college counselors can no longer spend the time necessary to get to know individual students like they might have done in decades past. A school which might have boasted a staff of six or eight guidance or college counselors could now have a staff of only two, three, or four counselors.

Additionally, more is expected from guidance and college counselors than ever before. In addition to managing the college application process and doing so for a far larger percentage of students than in decades past, counselors must often also work with special education departments on an increasing quantity of individualized education plans and the accompanying accommodations, registration concerns, and disciplinary issues.

With their caseload doubled and their workload increased by far more than just mere numbers college counselors are no longer able to guide students through the college application process as closely as they would like to.

School administrators have dealt with overcrowded and underfunded schools for decades. Despite that, our school systems continue to innovate and look for new ways to educate students regardless of increased pressure and oversight.

Teachers perform nothing short of miracles with fewer and fewer resources for more and more students. They achieve successful results despite societal pressure, which puts more blame on them in exchange for less respect.

An area which has fallen behind is support for programs that build test-taking and study skills. Schools are currently very good at building knowledge. When students put in the work, giving teachers the attention and respect they deserve, they will finish a high school career with a strong knowledge base in language arts, math, science, and social studies. High school students can expect to enter college with a knowledge base that will set them up for success dealing with college-level material.

However, high school students struggle with other aspects of college. They lack a strong base of skills in preparing for tests, writing efficiently when confronted with an extemporaneous topic, decoding confusing questions, and analyzing dense texts. This program begins the process that will help students master those skills.

Historically, test prep programs offered by high schools, whether public, charter, or private, have tended to fail because teachers, counselors, and administrators have focused on revisiting the academic content within the SAT or ACT. This fails because it doesn't actually address what the SAT and ACT are testing. They are not tests of knowledge but of critical thinking and decision-making under pressure.

Administrators, counselors, and teachers can utilize this book to build a successful test prep program that is effective, cost-efficient, and flexible. The best piece of advice I can give to educators is that they should trust the process and trust themselves. They have already provided a knowledge base that their students need to do well on the SAT or ACT. Now is the time to broaden the instruction to encompass analytical reading, critical thinking, and problem-solving skills that will help students improve their results on the SAT or ACT and beyond.

NEXT STEPS

This book is a guide. You have to do the work, whether you are a student, parent, teacher, counselor, or school administrator. This includes doing all of the preparation necessary to ensure program success for the weeks, and sometimes years, before an SAT or ACT program begins. Clearly, the first time you hack an SAT or ACT program into existence you will most likely be doing so with barely enough time to complete the program before your targeted test date, but use that first attempt as a tool for learning how to do it better next time. And then the time after that. Especially for schools and nonprofit organizations, our hope is that you build up a real program that can help students for years to come.

Furthermore, while the goal is to hack an SAT or ACT program into being while spending as little money as possible, you may need to spend some money. There are quite a few resources available for free, especially on the internet. You'll frequently utilize resources you already have, such as teaching spaces, seating, and other tools. But some things just cost money, such as printing paper and educational supplies. Hopefully you can reduce the cost, but be aware of this old adage: you'll only get as much out of this as you put into it.

Given what has been happening over the last year, with the advent of the novel coronavirus and the rapid transition to social distancing, remote learning and work, and heavy use of online resources, it is more important than ever for students, parents, educators, and administrators to look for ways to hack a successful test prep program into existence. At Livius, we have addressed this radical change by quickly pivoting all of our test prep programs, including private tutoring, classes, and informational meetings, to online programs. This is not so different from public and private K-12 schools and colleges across the country.

There are multiple video chat and digital whiteboard platforms available for instructors and students to use, and they all have their positives and negatives. The most important factor to consider is that students have live, in-person guidance through the test prep and college admissions process. Online instruction is now a reality for most students in the United States and across the world, however, it is only as effective as the program, curriculum, and instructor.

Chapter 2

THE BUYER'S GUIDE ON SAT/ACT TEST PREP OPTIONS

There are many options for test prep available, from online to in-center to after-school programs. With so many options, it can feel overwhelming to know what to look for when evaluating a program, especially in order to find one that's the best fit for your child. This chapter will serve as a buyer's guide of sorts to help you understand what to look for when considering test prep options.

To really understand how these services work, it helps to know where the industry itself got started, as well as how it's changed over time.

HOW THE TUTORING AND TEST PREP INDUSTRY HAS CHANGED

Let's jump in the time machine and travel back to the second century BC, when a man by the name of Livius Andronicus thrived writing poems, comedies, and even translating famous Greek works like the *Odyssey* into Latin. Today he's referred to as the founder of Latin literature.[1]

What many people don't know is that Livius was born into slavery. He spent much of his earlier years in service to a Roman noble family. Livius leveraged his substantial writing talents to create curricula that could be used to educate this family. He worked with each of the family members individually to support their educational growth. His tutoring work eventually earned him his freedom, and from there he went on to write some of history's most recognized classical plays.

Now let's move a little forward in time. In 1946, after World War II, there was a dramatic rise in students matriculating to college. While the SAT had already been around for twenty years by that point, never before had there been such demand to take the exam. Test preparation was virtually nonexistent in much of the country at the time. However, in New York City, a businessman by the name of Stanley Kaplan launched a tutoring business that claimed to raise student scores by one hundred points. The Federal Trade Commission ended up investigating his claims, ruling in the end that the average increase was more like twenty-five points, but that his methods did, in fact, increase scores. From there, demand for his services skyrocketed. This eventually led to the Kaplan Test Prep we know today.[2]

Thousands of years after early academic creators like Livius, the need for personalized education remains. The last few decades have shown the monetization of this demand, with the tutoring industry exploding into one of the fastest-growing business models in our

---

1   "Lucius Livius Andronicus," *Encyclopædia Britannica*, accessed May 15, 2020, https://www.britannica.com/biography/Lucius-Livius-Andronicus.

2   Patricia Sullivan, "Test-Preparation Pioneer Kaplan, 90, Dies," *Washington Post*, August 25, 2009.

economy. And it's expected to maintain that growth, with some estimates surpassing $120 billion by 2021.[3]

In many ways, this is great news for parents, because it means there are a bevy of options to choose from. With growth, however, come concerns about accountability. As in any industry, there are people who prey on the fears of the consumer, offering guarantees, false promises, and unsavory practices that border on cheating. One aim of this buyer's guide is to arm readers with knowledge so they can make informed decisions about the best kind of test prep for their child or themselves.

On the other hand, test preparation and tutoring have made significant positive developments in the last few decades, particularly in the last ten years. Perhaps the most noteworthy development is that with our progress in online learning, it's never been easier to find high-quality and affordable options for tutors, no matter where you live.

To start, let's take a look at the different tutoring programs available to students today.

TYPES OF PROGRAMS

There are three major program types to consider when you're seeking test prep for the SAT or ACT:

1. Private Tutoring: In this arrangement, a student and a tutor work in a one-to-one setting to focus on individual academic needs as they relate to the subject being studied. Private tutoring is always live but can be done online or in person.

---

3   "Online Tutoring Services Forecasted to Be $120 Billion Dollar Industry by 2021," openPR, last modified June 17, 2019, https://www.openpr.com/news/1776517/online-tutoring-services-forecasted-to-be-120-billion-dollar-industry-by-2021.html.

2. <u>Group Classes</u>: Group classes are the most traditional and cost-effective format for SAT preparation. Classes range from a handful of students to fifty or more.

3. <u>Independent Study</u>: With access to online programs and curriculum, independent study has never been easier. If you have the motivation and determination to study on your own, this is a flexible and affordable educational option. For example, you can use this book as a guide to help you create your own program. We won't offer an in-depth exploration of independent study in this chapter, however. While they can be successful for a very specific type of student, they often can't offer the same benefits as live tutoring and classes.

There are variations among these three main categories, such as hybrid programs or small-group tutoring, but the programs above are the most commonly used by students, and they're the foundation upon which any other types of programs are based.

A WORD ABOUT ONLINE PROGRAMS

Before we get to the evaluation criteria, it's important to understand what *online* really means. Online is its own category of tutoring, though online offerings can also be a part of any type of program listed above.

Within the umbrella of online tutoring, there are two types of programs, asynchronous and synchronous. Asynchronous online programs are ones that do not involve set instruction times, and rather than live, responsive tutoring, they use prerecorded videos or a self-led program to deliver content.

Asynchronous programs typically require students to work independently through a course at their own pace. This means students will be on their own during the instruction—watching, reading, completing practice questions and exams, and absorbing information as best as they can. Conversely, because students are 100 percent in charge of their own schedules, these programs are extremely flexible, which some families may find to be a perk.

These programs can work well for some students, but unfortunately the completion rate tends to be fairly low. Considering the individual student, their schedule, cost, and motivation to complete a self-led program should all be weighed when looking into this option. Will a lack of immediate, live support play a factor in your child's ability to complete an asynchronous test prep course?

Alternatively, synchronous online programs take place around a schedule of live events, usually including support or instruction from a live tutor. This live interaction can occur in group or one-to-one sessions and sometimes may even take place in person as a supplement to a self-led course (this would be a hybrid test prep option). Asynchronous programs that add in a synchronous element of live tutoring can be extremely successful and see much better results than an asynchronous program alone.

Another important note after working in test prep for many years is this: as long as you have a well-trained tutor, it's abundantly clear that one-to-one live tutoring is equally effective in both in-person and online learning environments. In fact, due to the high level of engagement, responsiveness, and personalized learning, we consider any one-to-one live tutoring to be the best option for students, whether that session is taking place in person or online. This may be a surprising stance, but it's one we've arrived at carefully.

The biggest concern we see parents raise with online instruction is the lack of an authentic relationship between the provider and the client. Not necessarily between the tutor and the student (which varies), but between the family and the provider itself. Often parents find that they feel anonymous, and that the experience is cookie cutter in nature, lacking in individualization.

Here's why this might happen: with less overhead for online programs, providers can charge much less. This is good news for parents who find they're priced out of in-person tutoring, whether center-based or in-home. However, in some cases, the lower cost can lead bigger providers to turn online programs into a numbers game. When the aim is to serve as many students as possible in order to positively affect revenue, service can really suffer as a result.

This means it's important to find an online test prep provider that's truly aligned around many of the same core tenets of quality in-person instruction. These include personalization of test prep, meaningful student engagement, and authentic relationship building with both the student and the family.

If you're deciding if an online program is right for you and your child, you'll need to weigh the pros and cons and look closely at what the program offers, both in terms of support and instruction. With a strong online program, you can get an affordable choice that truly does a great job in a one-to-one setting. And don't worry—an online tutor, when well trained, can help a student stay engaged even from the other side of a computer screen or device. So much about the quality and outcome of your tutoring program depends on the tutor themselves, just as it does with an in-person program.

With online programs, you need to ask questions early and often, and you need to know what you're looking for. For example, how necessary is an interactive experience? How much individual support do you expect your child to receive? How much training do you want the teacher or tutor to have? How much does cost factor into your decision? How much time remains before the next SAT exam? What's the best learning environment for your child? Be clear about your own expectations from the get-go, and you won't be disappointed.

Regardless of whether you're seeking out an in-person or online option, if at all possible, look for a one-to-one tutoring opportunity— chances are you'll be pleasantly surprised to see how effective and successful online tutoring programs can be.

EVALUATION CRITERIA

What should you look for when deciding if a program is the right fit? Here's our list of evaluation criteria for finding the ideal match for your student's needs and goals.

Instructors/Tutors

Tutors come from a variety of academic and instructional backgrounds. Because of that, they will have different strengths in terms of communication, ability to explain concepts, warmth, engagement with students, and so forth. It can seem daunting when you first begin your search, but don't panic. You can almost always find someone who is a good fit for your child if you're ready to spend the time researching and interviewing. Another area to expect variability? Cost. The hourly price ranges from $40 to $10,000. Yes, seriously!

Individual freelance tutors are often the least expensive option, but you may find in this case that you get what you pay for. They might be good, or even great. But the challenge with an individual tutor who isn't connected to a center or company is that they have to run their business on their own. Most critically, this means there isn't the same oversight when it comes to academic rigor. College entrance exams are complicated and frequently changing in terms of content and structure. Is a freelance tutor up to date on these changes? How can you be sure?

In addition, a freelance tutor also has to keep up with the demands of their business, which means running all of the customer service, scheduling, and invoicing. While this is enterprising (and plenty of freelance tutors do excellent work), it also means you may end up working with someone who isn't as organized or focused as you'd like. Partnering with a tutor from a testing company *at the very least* allows the tutor to focus on what they do best: teaching. They don't have to worry about research and development, marketing, sales, or anything else.

That said, a freelance tutor is definitely better than not using a tutor at all! If you choose that route, consider the following:

- You aren't going to be sure about major changes in the tests unless you research them yourself, so do your homework and ask your tutor about your findings.
- Referrals are critical. They indicate the tutor has connected well with previous students, helped them achieve their goals, and were engaging enough to inspire someone to recommend them to others. A good personal referral is truly a golden ticket in this situation, so ask around.
- Ask the tutor for recommendations of their own, and then call those families to ask about their experience. The most important question to ask is this: Was this tutor personally connected with your child and invested in their success?

Tutors within an established program will usually cost more. Again, you get what you pay for in this case as well. That extra per-hour fee means the tutor has been vetted for you, so it can be easier to find engaged, up-to-date instructional experts in the field. Provided you're working with a high-quality test prep business that values the interpersonal factor of tutoring, hiring a tutor through a dedicated test prep company means that there's quality assurance in place, as well as up-to-date training. A great company will recruit great tutors and do everything in their power to keep them on staff.

Many places hire tutors with previous experience in the field, allowing a sort of "tenure," or industry longevity, to act as a first step in the vetting process. Tutors who know the tests and who have years of experience helping students dive into the information and develop skills and strategies are also most often the same tutors whose interpersonal skills and academic know-how shine. These are the cream of the crop that high-quality test prep companies are seeking out.

When looking at tutors who work within a company, be sure to ask the sales representative specific questions related to training:

What training do you provide for your tutors?
The right answer: We provide [X] hours of both academic/curriculum training (hard skills) and interpersonal training (soft skills). Truth be told, what falls in that X spot isn't all that important. The exact number of hours is less significant than the fact that planning and implementation has been considered regarding both of these aspects of teaching.

How do you teach your tutors those important soft skills?
The right answer: We encourage our tutors to first engage in active listening. If asked, our tutors should be able to meaningfully tell us about their students. What colleges are they interested in? What movies do they like? What activities do they participate in? This is

usually an easy way to tell where a tutor falls on the line regarding their ability to foster a relationship with a student. Often, just asking them to learn about their students can help guide them toward creating more meaningful connections that are an important part of the learning process.

Note: It can be hard for companies to spend time and money on training for both hard skills AND soft skills, especially because teaching soft skills can be more of a nuanced conversation versus a standard practice. In many cases, this is why companies will lean on tenure and previous industry experience when they make a hire. They're operating under the assumption that after a certain number of years in the field, most tutors who lack these interpersonal skills won't still be around.

Do you have expert or master-level tutors?

The right answer: Our master-level tutors have at least five thousand hours of experience.

Note: You will pay a premium for this level of experience, and it will be worth it! It's proof that the tutor is exceptionally good at building a relationship with students, engaging them in instruction, and achieving results.

In the end, the best way to know if a tutor is right for your child is to schedule a one-time meeting. Ask for a free trial, if possible. If that isn't an option, then ask if you're able to pay for only a single session. If the company insists on a package deal, then at the very least there must be a policy in place to get your money back or switch tutors until a good match is found. If a company won't make these kinds of allowances, then it's probably a sign they aren't using adequate standards for hiring and retaining their tutors.

CURRICULUM

Here's one of the industry's best-kept secrets: everyone has a secret strategy! Or so they say. . . .

Most companies will try to sell you on the idea that they have the "secret sauce." They alone have the magical formula to ensure your child's success. But if you look at them side by side, the strategies from one company to another are actually quite similar. At Livius, for example, we utilize a strategy called the Zig Zag Method. It's an excellent strategy, but there are other companies out there that follow a similar instructional path—they just call it something a little different. There might be minor changes or nuances in application between the strategies, and those seemingly minor differences certainly can create a lightbulb moment for one student over another—we don't want to discount that. But at the end of the day, there's a finite number of strategies you can really use for these tests. If someone is telling you they have the one true and singular method for success, either they're lying or they're wrong.

So, what exactly is curriculum? And what should parents be looking for in terms of strategies?

Curriculum is the content being taught. It includes the strategies, methods, and tools your child will learn and internalize. This is the critical toolbox a student takes with them into the testing room. No matter what a company names their strategies, if they've taken the time to develop them and have data to back up their success, it's a promising sign for parents who want quality instruction. If you ask for a company's *proven strategies for success*, they should be able to specifically describe these tools and prove their effectiveness with numbers.

You might be thinking, "But don't all testing preparation companies have strategies?" Sadly, no. Many companies use a "drill and kill" method of instruction instead. Under this model, the tutor will give a student a practice test, and then after the test is complete, the tutor will go through the questions and answers. That's the entire model. They simply go through the practice questions over and over. And while it's true that some practice is better than nothing at all, this method is deeply flawed in that it gives the students no actual tools and so, of course, yields far fewer positive results.

Strategies are specific, and they should empower students. The student will take these tools and work through the material, build on their test-taking skills, and practice in a way that encourages continued skill development. When interviewing companies, ask the salesperson, "Can you give me an example of a strategy you teach, or can you talk to me more about what's included in your curriculum?"

In later chapters of this book, we provide examples of specific strategies for students to learn and implement. Use this as a model for what type of information to look for when vetting a test prep company about their curriculum.

Choosing Providers: Local versus National

Local providers have bigger overheads, but their service is often at a much higher level than national brands. These smaller businesses (mostly mom-and-pop type of shops) see the student as an individual. They usually take more time per student and get to know them and you as well. They're typically invested in the success of each student who comes through their doors, which means they're responsive and willing to go the extra mile when necessary.

Larger national brands, however, are more likely to view each student as a number. They don't need your money or business, specifically. The stakes just aren't as high for them, so there will be less individualization and flexibility when it comes to meeting the student's needs.

Your third option of an online provider is much more affordable . . . but you have to understand what you're getting, because they aren't all created equally.

Sometimes the academic rigor of a reputable national brand is worth the trade-off in terms of relationship development, customer service, and commitment to the student's success. This is an individual decision to make, and you can narrow down your choices using some of the questions and considerations we've outlined across this chapter.

Format of Instruction

Hours, preassessments, class size. The format for test prep instruction is important. The number of hours of instruction, for example, is the first thing most parents look at. The bigger the package (the higher the number of hours), the better value you get. That's true across the board.

However, you should beware of overkill. Once you pass around thirty hours of private tutoring, there's not much left to cover. Outside of unique situations where a student has large academic gaps to try and cover, you typically won't need a tutoring package that's more than thirty hours, at most. And the timing of those hours also matters—it would be a waste to use all of those hours before the first exam. Instead, it's better to break up sessions across multiple test dates. This means a student will participate in their tutoring programs for a certain number of hours, then sit for the exam, then return for more tutoring based on their biggest areas of opportunity. This allows for more meaningful and responsive learning.

Where does score choice factor into all of this? Score choice allows the best test scores to be sent to schools no matter how many times the exam has been taken. This provides a unique opportunity to use private tutoring to pinpoint areas of weakness and practice to elevate skill.

By staggering your package of tutoring hours before and after taking an exam, a student can often drive a more significant score increase.

For this reason, it might be a waste to buy a large package of thirty or more hours up front, before even taking the exam. You get more bang for your buck if you use preassessment, then targeted instruction, and finally more pinpointed instruction after sitting for the exam. This method of layering has a powerful impact. Consider all of this when deciding on what type of experience you want for your student.

One-on-one: We can't emphasize this enough—always choose individual private tutoring when you can. There are PLENTY of one-on-one options out there that cost the same as a small group or a larger class. To keep sessions affordable, this may mean that you seek out one-to-one online tutoring. Remember that online tutoring can be just as good as in-person tutoring. It's the individualization that makes the magic.

Small group (this may look like six-to-one or three-to-one): If you can't get one-on-one, this is your next best option. Your student will get more attention and support in a small group setting rather than a larger class.

Classes: If your student must take a class, take note that they should NEVER be in a class program with more than fifteen students. That's the absolute max that we recommend. Even the most talented, devoted instructor can't provide the level of individual attention required for a class program to be successful with more than fifteen students in attendance.

Pricing

The cost of instruction varies based on in-center, online, and independent models.

In-Center:

The price for in-center instruction will almost always be higher than the other options. Your student will be learning in a safe, comfortable environment that's optimized for learning. Understandably, there's a premium associated with that. With this option, you also get the benefit of a center director who's focused on ensuring students are engaged and learning, that tutors are excelling in their instruction, and that parents are happy. In-center tutoring allows for better tutor matching, more comprehensive relationship building, and the development of a sense of community. All of these factors impact your student's confidence and comfort. It also impacts your student's test scores.

Online Tutoring:

With online learning, you won't pay for the physical learning environment, so the cost will inherently be less. However, you're still paying for a tutor who's vetted, trained, and operating according to a set curriculum. With a good company, they'll be using a reliable methodology even if there's less in-person interaction. With the right provider, online tutoring can really be a best-of-both-worlds solution for parents and students.

Independent Tutoring:

This is usually the most affordable option by a large margin, and it does offer both convenience and some specific flexibility. Tutors might come right to your house, for example. However, as we've mentioned—you get what you pay for. It's very difficult to vet independent tutors. Is this tutor truly aware of the best strategies or most recent test changes? If so, you might get the best tutor of your life! If not, it might be a disaster. And you might not know that until you've already spent a lot of time and money investing in the process.

A Word about Guarantees

Most in-center programs offer some type of guarantee, as do some online providers. There's more to this than you may expect, though. Money-back guarantees sound good, but they often come with very strict and hard-to-achieve stipulations. A repeat of the class is the more common and straightforward guarantee.

Guarantees sound good, and if your student completes a program and scores *lower* than their initial test score, we've found that guarantees will be honored pretty consistently. While this may sound reassuring, the reality is that if a student follows the program, puts in the effort, goes to the sessions, and does the homework, that hard work will almost always lead to an improved score. Because of this general consistency, it's not exactly a big risk on the company's side to offer a guarantee if there isn't any score improvement.

If you're using a guarantee as part of your method for vetting a company, start by reading the fine print. For some companies, the stipulations are extremely specific. For example, your student might be required to take a branded preassessment on a specific day, or to start with a certain score. Many of the national programs have these types of requirements for any guarantee to be honored.

Finally, note that for most guarantees, you'll find that the higher the initial test score, the harder it is to guarantee improvement. If your child is starting off in the eightieth to eighty-fifth percentile (which is a score of around 1,240 for the SAT or above a 25 for the ACT) there can still be plenty of value in tutoring. But because the improvement may not be as dramatic, many companies will not offer a guarantee at that point (or, if they do, it won't be in the form of money back).

Questions to Ask All Providers

The best way to vet a company and to discover if they're the right fit is with an initial consultation during which you can ask questions and feel out the overall ethos and approach. The best way to do that is to come with a handful of questions that can help illuminate a business's practices.

For one-on-one tutors, ask all the following questions:

Which test should my student take?
This is one of the most important questions you can ask, and it's a great way to immediately rule out a company that isn't operating with your student's best interest at heart. Students should not ever prepare for both exams.

When you ask this question, the answer needs to include some level of acknowledgment that the SAT and the ACT are each better suited to specific learning styles, which means test prep should almost always start with some type of process for figuring out which exam is the best fit for an individual student.

For this reason, the answer to this question will tell you right away if a test prep company or tutor truly understands the testing process and the value of individualizing instruction. Many companies see the confusion around the SAT and ACT as an opportunity to exploit consumers. They advise students to prep for both tests, which is very expensive for parents and very stressful and time consuming for students. It's a bad idea all around. If someone tries to sell you on the necessity of preparing for both exams, run in the other direction.

Instead, work only with a company that understands the tests and is willing to advise your student regarding which specific test they should take and why. The answer will depend on the student as an individual. A good company will work with you and your student to figure this out.

How do you track students' results?
If a company advertises success data, such as a guaranteed two-hundred-point score increase, then this question also tells you about the actual value of that guarantee.

Look for a tutoring company that has a systematic process in place for following up with students after tutoring so they can track their data. If the company doesn't know the answer to this question or they don't have a standard system for tracking results—this is also a red flag.

What are the criteria for score guarantees?
As we noted above, this is your chance to take a magnifying glass to the fine print. Look closely and see how transparent the requirements are and ask for clarification around any stipulations.

How do you match tutors?
When finding the best fit between a student and an instructor, a company should be evaluating all or most of the following: learning style, availability, prior tutoring experience, the type of teacher they best respond to and why, and, finally, what they're engaged with beyond the classroom (such as extracurricular activities, hobbies, passions, etc.). These questions show that a genuine effort is being made to ensure

a student is going to work with someone who has the best chance of motivating them, teaching them, and developing a quality relationship with them.

For a small group or class, ask all of the above, and then also ask for the following information:

- *How many hours is your class/program?*
- *What is the minimum and maximum class size?*
- *What happens to a student if the class isn't run? Will there be a makeup class? Will I receive my money back?*
- *How do you select the instructors?*
- *What is an expected amount of time for my student to get a question answered? (For example, is there a twenty-four-hour response policy regarding emailed questions?)*

At the end of the day, while there isn't necessarily a perfect "right" answer to these questions, what you're really looking for is transparency. A legitimate provider will be eager to explain their process. By asking these questions, you can figure out pretty quickly if someone is hiding a deficiency with marketing and gimmicks.

Choosing the Right Path for Your Needs

Transparency. Individualization. Engagement.

The right program for your child is the one that meets your child's needs. Some students work better in a room designed for instruction, with a tutor sitting next to them. Some students work better in their bedroom on their laptop. This decision is personal, and the right answer for one family will be wrong for the next.

However, we do know ALL students work better with one-on-one support. ALL students work better with a flexible, individualized method of instruction that incorporates proven strategies. ALL students need to feel engaged while they're learning and to feel like what they're doing matters. And all parents need to be able to trust the learning process, so they know their money (and their child's time) is being well spent.

A good program employs sales representatives who are knowledgeable and ready to talk about all aspects of the program. There shouldn't be any hemming and hawing, anything hidden or lacking in transparency. Sales representatives should be educators themselves, people who understand the commitment that families are making, as well as the commitment that the *company* is making to its clients.

As you vet programs to find the right match, ask questions. If something isn't clear, ask for clarification. Ask for referrals. The only way to assure a good testing result for your child is to start the whole process with their needs at the forefront. You should expect a well-matched tutor and a program set up for their success. Your student deserves nothing less.

Chapter 3

SHOULD YOU TAKE THE SAT OR ACT?

The first question that many parents ask me when they discover I am a test prep tutor is, "Should my child take the SAT or ACT?" This question is relatively new in the college admissions process. During the twentieth century, colleges and universities accepted either the SAT or the ACT, never both, and the answer was simple. Now that colleges accept both relatively equally, the answer is less simple.

To answer the question of which test you should take during the college admissions process, we have to understand what is different about the two tests. The most recent versions of the SAT and the ACT, which both underwent updates of varying degrees in 2016, are more similar in structure and format than they have ever been. Yet, there are still large and important differences between the tests. Those differences can be summed up in the philosophies of the two tests.

The SAT is a thinking test, and it always has been. From the beginning, the SAT has promised to predict college readiness and college performance by testing a student's aptitude for college. The use of the word *aptitude* is very revealing. The idea was that some students are just predisposed to college success while others are not. This has since been proven to be false, of course. Any student, regardless of their background, socioeconomic status, or upbringing, can succeed in college, provided they find the right support and program.

With that philosophy in mind, the SAT is designed to test a student's critical thinking and analytical reading skills under timed pressure. Each question on the SAT, whether it is in a reading, writing, or math section, presents you with a word problem which must be interpreted and dissected in order to be solved. In other words, every SAT question is an inference question.

An inference is made when a person encounters information and then must make an intuitive leap to figure out a missing piece of information based on the clues or hints provided in the text, image, or data. Knowledge is useful in making an inference, but problem-solving skills are essential.

The College Board, the makers of the SAT, have claimed for years that it is a mischaracterization to call the SAT a puzzle test, but that is exactly what it is. Each question is a small puzzle based on the information provided and utilizing the student's pool of knowledge as the cost of entry into the puzzle. In other words, a vocabulary word, grammar concept, or math skill can keep you from solving a question on the SAT, but knowing these things is not enough to successfully answer SAT questions. You must use your knowledge as one factor in beating the puzzle that each question presents.

The ACT, by contrast, is designed as a test of showing off what you know. The ACT organization, which has the same name as the test, was founded on the idea that academic skill and raw knowledge are the best indicators of future success in college. The writers of the ACT have designed the test to allow students to demonstrate their skill in reading, grammar, and math, utilizing the pool of knowledge they have constructed over their high school careers.

ACT questions tend to be far more straightforward in structure. These questions require you to identify details in the reading passage, grammar passages, scientific data sets, and math questions. Then you are asked to "solve" the question utilizing that information.

At first blush, ACT questions can seem easier than SAT questions. ACT passages and questions are densely packed with information, but they generally avoid inferences, focusing instead on identifying details and solving relatively clearly written questions. Many of the students with whom I have worked over the years have stated that, individually, ACT questions feel easier to them, but students do not work on ACT questions individually. They complete them in timed sections.

The ACT increases the difficulty level of the test by imposing a draconian time limit on students. The SAT, and other standardized tests, have time limits as well, but the time limit on the ACT is considered by observers (such as myself) to be the most intense and unforgiving. As we dive into the strategies later in the book, I will go into more detail on the specific sections in the two tests; however, at this point it should suffice to say that students generally receive about one-third less time per question on the ACT as compared to the SAT.

Time is the other big difference between the two tests. While the rest of the world of education has deemphasized the importance of time limits, the SAT and the ACT have maintained time's influence on student results. In Massachusetts, for example, students take a yearly test beginning in third grade called the MCAS. In my time as a middle school math teacher, I had the opportunity to administer MCAS to my homeroom students. The test, like all state testing, is designed to gauge student progress and mastery of skills taught over the previous year. Technically, the test has a time limit; however, since the goal of the test is to identify what each student has learned over the last year, not how fast a student works, students can take extra time as needed. In fact, students who need extra time can work throughout the school day to complete the test.

Most jobs that adults have in life do not impose strict time limits. Whether a person works in academic, business, legal, or medical fields, few jobs really require highly condensed time periods in order to accomplish tasks. There are jobs like that in the world, but far fewer than jobs that don't do so. The MCAS, and other state tests, reflect the truth that, most of the time, people have the time they need to do their jobs.

By comparison, the SAT and the ACT are strictly timed down to the second. This type of strict timing provides a major factor in the SAT or ACT experience: time pressure. Both tests depend on time pressure as part of their metrics for college readiness, but the ACT utilizes time pressure as a tool for increasing difficulty as well.

The third major difference between the two tests is the essay. At this point, many of the readers might object, recognizing that the essays on both the SAT and the ACT are optional for students. While it is true that fewer and fewer colleges and universities require students to submit an essay score during the admissions process, a large number of colleges accept the essay score.

Regardless of how important the essay may be, it provides another point of comparison between the SAT and the ACT. Once again, the philosophical differences between the College Board and the ACT organization are laid bare in the essay portion of both tests.

The SAT essay is an analytical writing exercise. Students are presented with a two-plus-page-long passage which they must read and then analyze. The passage is either an article written by a professional journalist published by a legitimate news source which the College Board has licensed or an excerpt from a historically relevant speech or essay by a well-known public figure. You are tasked with analyzing the effectiveness and persuasiveness of the writer's argument.

The ACT essay is more similar to what the majority of students write in English language arts classes in high school. It is a hybrid of a persuasive essay utilizing the student's own opinions and an analytical essay. Students encounter a short paragraph on a current issue, one which the students might have encountered previously in their own studies or lives. They are then provided three differing opinions, or Perspectives, on the issue. The task is to write an essay in which students state their own opinion on the issue, defending that position with one or more clear and specific examples, as well as analyzing one or more of the Perspectives in terms of their own opinions.

Once again, the SAT asks students a complex question requiring them to go beyond what they've learned in school. The SAT essay is a writing puzzle. Can they figure out what is in the passage in terms of the techniques and concepts utilized by the author?

The ACT essay, by contrast, is a far more straightforward task. Responding to a small, common issue of the day, can students clearly state an opinion, defend it, and then use it to relate to other opinions on that issue?

Most of the students with whom I have worked have told me that they find the ACT essay easier, however this does not mean that students invariably score higher on the ACT essay than the SAT essay.

Easier doesn't mean better. Just because a student understands the question better does not mean that they know the answer.

This brings us back to the initial question: should I take the SAT or the ACT? Given the differences between the two tests, the answer is not simple, and it is not universal. It all depends on one factor more than any other. Surprisingly, that factor is not academics. The two tests cover virtually identical content topics in reading, grammar, writing, and math, accounting for minor differences. Students who have taken more challenging classes in high school have a greater knowledge base to apply to either test; however, they can do so to either test equally.

Instead, the factor that best determines which test is best is personality. When students ask me which test they should take I always respond by asking students a question in return. I ask, "Do you like puzzles? Or would you prefer more straightforward questions, even if you get less time in which to answer them?"

That is the determining factor for me. A student who is not afraid of puzzles (not afraid of inferences, in other words) will already be better placed to do well on the SAT. A student who is not afraid of the time limit, on the other hand, will already be more likely to do well on the ACT.

Unfortunately, many students aren't sure about where their strengths lie. Many students, even those who perform well in school, have no idea if they like puzzles or not. Many students have not encountered strict time limits, especially considering the lack of time limits on state testing over the last decade. Many students just can't answer the question I ask them when they want to know which test to take.

Luckily, there are ways for students to get their answers. One is previous test scores. The vast majority of high schools in the United States, whether public or private, offer either the PSAT or the PreACT each

October to their junior class. In fact, for these students, the PSAT/PreACT is a requirement. Additionally, more and more high schools are requiring their students to take the PSAT/PreACT sophomore year as well. A small, but slowly growing, number of schools have students take both a PSAT and a PreACT, either in the same year or in consecutive years.

High schools use the data provided by the PSAT and/or the PreACT for a variety of purposes. In many states, for example, high schools are required to report these scores as one of many metrics on which the schools are judged by the state. The College Board encourages high schools to use sophomore PSAT results as a pretest for admission into Advanced Placement classes.

Since most high school juniors have taken at least one PSAT or PreACT, they can use these results, and their experiences on test day, to help them determine which test provides them with a better chance of achieving score goals. If a student has already taken a test, they probably have a good idea of how well they will do on future iterations.

Additionally, students can sign up for an actual SAT or ACT prior to starting a test prep program. This will provide students with a real score to use as a baseline for gauging improvement. Many students and parents are wary of this path because they are afraid that a low initial score will be counted against students during the college application process by college admissions officers. Luckily, this is not the case, as I will explain in further detail later in chapter 5.

Finally, you can take a full-length practice test. Taking a practice test is probably the most convenient option for most students, their families, and schools, since they can be administered any day of the week, regardless of the College Board or ACT organization schedule. Unfortunately, they can also be inaccurate. Unless the person administering the test (which means timing the sections and reading the directions to the students taking the practice test) follows the timing religiously and provides a quiet, secluded location for the test, the results can be affected.

A student interested in deciding between the SAT and the ACT has another factor to consider. Taking an actual SAT and ACT, or practice tests for both the SAT and ACT, requires a student to take twice as many tests to answer one question. If possible, you, or a school building their own SAT or ACT program, should take a comparison test. A comparison test is a single test with both short SAT sections and short ACT sections that easily compares performance on both tests. While neither the College Board nor the ACT organization offers such a test, many independent tutoring companies, including our own company, Livius, have created comparison tests. Understandably, creating a comparison test requires a serious commitment of time and resources, so we do not expect individual students and families, or even school districts, building their own SAT or ACT programs to do this.

One last factor can help a student, family, or school district determine which test is best for them. Historically, the SAT and the ACT were preferred by colleges and universities in different regions of the country. Even to this day, for example, the ACT organization writes and administers yearly state testing in several states. If your school district only administers the PSAT to juniors every year, or conversely only administers the PreACT to juniors every year, then you may not need to decide. The rest of your school's curriculum may be set up to guide you into taking one test over the other anyway.

Regardless of all of these factors, the decision of whether to take the SAT or the ACT is a personal one. My entire career has focused on helping students achieve their goals of gaining admission to the college of their choice, and whatever path helps them do that is the correct path. A student or a school district may try different things to help figure out which test gives students the best chance at reaching their goals, but the good news is that either test is currently acceptable to all of the colleges in the United States. Once you make a decision, you can't go wrong.

Chapter 4

THE HISTORY OF THE SAT AND THE ACT

Previously, I mentioned that during the twentieth century, colleges and universities only accepted one of the two tests during the admissions process. Now, of course, virtually every American college or university accepts either test equally. Why? What changed? Quite a bit, actually.

The story of why colleges and universities accept both the SAT and the ACT universally begins with the concept of standardized testing at the end of the nineteenth century. The end of the nineteenth century saw the founding of dozens of colleges and universities, both private and public, in states across the Union. As with many industries, there were very few requirements or regulations for starting a college or university, and the quality of the education provided by many of these newer institutions of higher learning varied wildly. During this period, organizations that accredited colleges and universities were founded to certify that these schools were legitimate.

The educational landscape was quite different in 1899 from what it is today. A person could still become a lawyer or a doctor by apprenticing with a professional and taking the bar or medical exams without attending college, much less graduate school. The majority of professionals, including the majority of US presidents, had not attended college through the end of the nineteenth century. In fact, according to the US Department of Education, less than 5 percent of all students both graduated high school and attended some level of college in the 1890s.

Up until this point, even long-established colleges and universities had widely varying standards for admissions, and the oldest universities often depended on family connections, what we would now call legacy admissions, to determine which students they would accept. In some ways, up until this point, colleges and universities had been expensive and exclusive finishing schools for the children of the wealthiest and most well-connected Americans.

Educational leaders at both the prestigious private high schools and reputable colleges and universities along the eastern seaboard saw an opportunity to take a larger role in determining qualifications for professional status in several professions, especially the legal and medical fields. Universities began to found law schools and medical schools in the post–Civil War period and designed comprehensive exams that were required for graduation.

Furthermore, during the post–Civil War period, dozens of land-grant colleges and universities were founded in western and southern states alongside a slew of private, religious colleges, which greatly expanded the number of institutions of higher learning from several hundred colleges in the United States as late as the 1850s to over 1,000 college and universities by 1899.

The College Board was founded in 1899 at Columbia University by representatives from a dozen universities and several private high schools to provide a series of standardized tests in various academic subjects which colleges and universities could use to gauge a student's knowledge during the admissions process. In order to provide a more standardized model for the admissions process, some of the leading lights at colleges and universities such as Columbia, Penn, NYU, Rutgers, Vassar, Princeton, Cornell, and Bryn Mawr worked together to design a set of exams that would prove a student's acumen in a variety of subjects, such as Latin, Greek, mathematics, history, botany, chemistry, English, French, physics, and several others. Thus, the College Entrance Examination Board (CEEB) was born.

The idea, of course, was that not only would the founding twelve colleges and universities utilize these exams, but that the exams would be made available to all colleges and universities, especially the newer schools, in order to establish a high standard of knowledge that all prospective candidates must achieve in order to be considered for admission to an institute of higher learning.

Although the College Entrance Examination Board later changed its name to the College Board, you can still see the remnants of the original name in the CEEB codes that are used to identify both specific colleges and universities and the various majors available at these colleges and universities when students fill out forms while taking the SAT or the SAT Subject Tests or during the college application process. The CEEB codes are used by high schools throughout the country and by third-party organizations, such as those that award scholarships. Interestingly, the ACT organization maintains its own codes for colleges and for majors, but it is less often used by outside organizations.

At first, only a small percentage of students took the CEEB's college boards, as they were called initially, and mostly only by students applying for admission to Columbia University. The original 1900 college boards required five days to complete and mostly consisted of essay questions. Over the next two decades as much as 10 percent of all students applying to college were taking the college boards, mostly for admission to prestigious private colleges and universities in the northeastern United States. Other colleges and universities, especially public institutions, began offering their own entrance exams, while many smaller, private colleges depended almost exclusively on letters of recommendation and interviews to ensure that students deserved admission.

The first two decades of the twentieth century also saw throughout the United States the founding of scores of "junior colleges," now mostly known as community colleges. The percentage of students graduating high school, applying for admission, and attending college doubled during this period. More and more students applied to colleges in their home states as satellite campuses broke away to become full colleges or universities in their own right. The prestigious schools of the Northeast also saw an increase in the number of students applying for admissions, including students from populations who had never previously applied to places like Harvard or Princeton: female, African American, and Jewish students.

It is at this point that the story of the College Board and higher education in the United States becomes uncomfortable. To fail to acknowledge the prejudices of people during this period in American history is to set up a situation in which we fail to address the same prejudices today. All of the institutions involved in this part of the story have evolved since this time, and I am in no way accusing them of racism, sexism, or anti-Semitism in their modern incarnations. Back in the 1920s, however, everything was a different story.

In order for the next part of the story to make sense, you have to remember that the CEEB's college board exams, and the similar exams administered locally by individual colleges and universities throughout the country, were knowledge-based tests. So long as a student had mastered a subject like Latin or biology, that student could theoretically pass the college board exam in that topic. That meant that students who were not generally considered for admission to many colleges or universities due to gender, religion, or race were passing the college board exams and demanding admissions.

This result was unacceptable to many in leadership at colleges and universities around the country. At the time, it was believed that women were supposed to go to women's colleges, that African American men were supposed to attend the "black land-grant colleges" or private historically Black colleges and universities (HBCU), and that the Jewish community should found their own Jewish colleges, rather than attempt to attend a college or university not meant for them. Furthermore, the women's colleges and HBCUs were considered nothing better than teacher training schools, far below the academic prestige of the top universities in the Northeast.

Regardless of the fact that female, African American, and Jewish students were now passing the college board exams that theoretically qualified them for admission to prestigious universities in what we now call the Ivy League, leaders at those schools did not believe that students in those communities had the appropriate aptitude to succeed at that level. What they needed was a way to prove their point.

The first widely available intelligence quotient test was developed by researchers for the US Army leading up to World War I. The idea was to help the army better place recently drafted soldiers into positions that best fit their intelligence. No one wanted to waste the brain of a soldier who could write or crack codes on a job in which he might be killed at the front, for example. Additionally, the army's intelligence quotient test was the first widely used multiple-choice test, reducing the amount of time it took a large organization such as the army to collect and collate results.

The CEEB hired the team of psychologists who developed the army's intelligence test to adapt it as a college admissions exam. The idea was to prove that individuals in certain groups, like white, Christian males, were more intelligent, and therefore more apt to succeed at a prestigious institution of higher learning, than individuals in other groups.

In 1926, the CEEB administered the Scholastic Aptitude Test (SAT) for the first time. Rather than the five days it took students to complete the college board exams, the original SAT took only four to five hours to complete. It consisted of nine sections, two math and seven verbal, scored on the familiar 200–800 scale with a mean of 500. The test was designed to determine a student's aptitude for college success based on the student's raw intelligence. It was predicted that this would weed out undesirable candidates, which essentially meant women and African American and Jewish men.

This plan, of course, failed miserably. Women scored just as well on the SAT as did men. African American and Jewish men scored just as well as white, Christian men. Many colleges and universities, especially the most prestigious and selective schools, later formalized bans on women in order to remain single-sex schools until the late 1960s. Colleges that had previously accepted an African American student here or there formalized bans that were not officially lifted until the late 1950s. Strict quotas reducing the number of Jewish men who could be admitted to Ivy League and other similar schools were put in place as well.

Only a handful of schools, mostly in the Ivy League, utilized the SAT at first, and generally as a supplement to the more traditional college board exams throughout the late 1920s and 1930s. In addition to using SAT results as a metric for admissions, many schools also began the tradition of using SAT results as a tool for determining academic or merit-based scholarship awards.

By the late 1930s, a large number of colleges and universities throughout the northeastern US, beyond the Ivy League, had begun to accept SAT scores to supplement the traditional college board exams or their own entrance exams, and more and more schools were accepting the SAT as a replacement for the traditional entrance exams. The SAT had many advantages over the days-long college board exams from CEEB or the individual entrance exams utilized by schools which did not accept the college boards. Not only could students complete the SAT in a matter of hours, but there were obvious benefits to the colleges. All college entrance exams were hand scored at this point, and an SAT could be scored in minutes, whereas the essay-based college board exams took almost as long to score as it took students to take the test.

Even before World War II, and the introduction of the GI Bill in 1944 that would dramatically increase the number of students applying to college by the 1950s, the factors that made the SAT more popular for students applying to college than the traditional college board exams convinced both colleges and universities and the CEEB to "suspend" the traditional college board exams in 1941. The SAT was now utilized by virtually every private college and university in the northeastern United States as a part of the admissions process.

Over the first thirty years of the SAT, the test writers at what was now called the College Board and the company that was founded to take over writing the questions, the Educational Testing Service (ETS), had gradually moved away from the original pure-puzzle questions based on the army's intelligence quotient test, and moved more toward reading, vocabulary, and math questions that depended on difficulty and skill. Even so, the SAT remained a "tricky" test that was supposed to identify the aptitude of the student for college success.

Even as late as 1958, only a handful of colleges and universities outside the northeastern United States (from Ohio eastward, from Maryland northward, and all throughout New England) utilized the SAT as part of their admission process. The majority of both public and private colleges and universities in the remainder of the country still depended on their own wildly varying entrance exams in the admissions process. Two professors at the University of Iowa saw an opportunity to simplify the entrance exam landscape and simultaneously strike a blow against what they saw as the elitist bias of the SAT and College Board toward traditional definitions of intelligence. The team at the newly founded American College Testing Inc. (ACT) instead designed a test, that they also called ACT, which would depend on learned knowledge and the ability to demonstrate that knowledge under timed conditions. They also promised that the results could be used for level placement within the various topics covered by the test.

For the first thirty years of the ACT's existence, the test consisted of an English (grammar and writing technique) section, a math section, a social studies section, and a natural sciences section. The ACT required the accumulation and memorization of a great deal of knowledge, and doing well on the test was a matter of demonstrating that knowledge in as quick and efficient a manner as possible within the time limit.

By the late 1960s, the higher education landscape had changed to resemble something more like what we see today. Virtually every college or university in the United States accepted either the SAT or the ACT as part of their admissions process, and locally designed and administered entrance exams had faded into history. Schools had fallen into two camps. Colleges in the Northeast still required the SAT. The University of California system, as well as private colleges along the West Coast, additional private colleges farther south along the Atlantic seaboard, and a handful of private colleges and universities in the South joined them. Colleges and universities, both public and private, in the central parts of the United States from Appalachia to the Rockies accepted the ACT. At this time, almost 60 percent of high school graduates took either the SAT or the ACT, yet only as much as 15 percent of high school graduates ever went on to college.

Despite both the slowly rising graduation rates at high schools and increasing enrollment in college by high school graduates during the 1970s and 1980s (which led to almost 25 percent of high school graduates attending college by 1991), stories of declining SAT scores, high dropout rates at both urban and rural high schools, and the mythical excellence of high schools in Japan, Scandinavia, and other locales across the globe created a sense of urgency for educational reform.

The early 1990s saw a major shift in education policy as national politicians saw the US Department of Education as a way for influencing the educational policies of the fifty states, which had been mostly left alone up until this point. The Department of Education had spent its existence as an agency which collected data on education in the United States. Now, the plan proposed by presidential candidate Bill Clinton was to use the Department of Education to build a system of grants and programs to affect education in the states. He made a campaign pledge that his policies would increase college enrollment from under 30 percent in 1992 to over 60 percent by 2009. Surprisingly, when George W. Bush was elected president in 2000, his education policies did not differ much from those of Bill Clinton, despite the two presidents hailing from opposing political parties. Bush's No Child Left Behind policies did add more testing and punishments for failing schools than Clinton's previous policies, but the grants and programs remained mostly the same.

The policy has been mostly successful. By 2010, almost 70 percent of high school graduates had attended some level of college. Additionally, the national dropout rate, which had actually dropped from 80 percent in 1940 to approximately 25 percent by the 1980s, had decreased further since then, with a national dropout rate of approximately 10 percent by 2010. And, for the first time, this rate was relatively consistent across all ethnic and racial group demographics. As this growth in high school graduation occurred, changes in the college admissions tests followed.

In the late 1980s and early 1990s, both the ACT and the SAT underwent updates that began the process of bringing them closer together in content and format. The ACT transformed the social studies section into the modern reading section, dropping the need to memorize facts about history, economics, and other topics, in favor of focusing on general reading skills utilizing texts in multiple topical areas. Additionally, the ACT natural science section became the science reasoning section. Once again, the need to memorize numerous science facts was replaced by a more logic-based approach. The new science section depended on graphs, tables, and charts to test students on their ability to use logic and reasoning, and a basic understanding of science concepts, to solve problems.

The SAT, by contrast, became somewhat less tricky of a test, switching, for example, the focus of the reading section from vocabulary puzzles, as it had been for over sixty years, to a section in which the majority of the questions were based on reading passages for the first time. The SAT math section shifted the focus of the multiple-choice portion by increasing the level of math skill required and eliminating some of the types of questions most mocked by teen movies in the 1980s. The SAT remained a tricky test that depended on memorization, however, with the reading section still consisting of almost 40 percent vocabulary puzzles and the math section including quantitative comparisons, a question type which asked students to compare the values of information in two columns. Quantitative comparison questions can still be found on the independent high school admittance test, the Independent School Entrance Exam (ISEE), as well as a few other smaller standardized tests.

This period of time also saw the College Board remove the grammar-based Test of Standard Written English (TSWE) from the SAT, although not the PSAT. Grammar-based questions were relegated to the Writing SAT II. Originally called the Achievement Tests when introduced in 1937 as the College Board's recommended exam for determining scholarship offers, by the 1980s the SAT IIs were used by the most competitive colleges and universities as a further tool in determining admission. In 2005 the tests would again be renamed to the current SAT Subject Tests. Interestingly, the grammar section and the essay introduced in the Writing SAT II would return to the SAT at this time.

Due to the rapid increase in the number of both high school graduates and students attending college, several unexpected effects arose. First, the number of students graduating high school and applying to college rapidly rose in response to the Clinton education policy and did so more quickly than anyone predicted.

Second, the number of students applying to colleges at distances farther away from home than ever before also rose rapidly. This was in response to a combination of factors. With more students applying to college, more of them looked away from home, especially to the oldest, most prestigious, and most competitive of colleges in the Northeast, for the first time. The other major factor was the rise of the internet and the birth of the World Wide Web. Students could now reach out to colleges that had previously seemed little more than myth through the power of email and the browser.

Third, the internet also created access for a new pool of international students who sought a new path to achieving the American Dream. While students from overseas had always been a part of the college landscape, they were historically more likely to attend American universities as graduate students. Starting in the 1990s, the number of international undergraduate applicants rose dramatically in line with the number of American high school graduate applicants.

The result was a huge increase in the number of applicants to colleges and universities across the United States, coupled with a smaller yet significant increase in the number of students accepted. An example I often use is that of Harvard University, since virtually everyone on the planet has heard of Harvard. In 1990, Harvard saw approximately five thousand high school graduates apply for approximately one thousand freshman spots. In 2017, Harvard saw approximately forty thousand high school graduates apply for two thousand freshman spots. While the number of students Harvard accepts for admission who matriculate as freshmen has literally doubled in twenty-eight years, the number of students applying has increased eightfold.

Yes, this is Harvard I am referencing, one of the most prestigious and famous universities on the planet. In addition, virtually every college and university across the United States, from the Ivy League to community colleges and everything in between, has seen their enrollment increase. In fact, it is more likely that any colleges that have failed and closed over the last two decades have done so not due to enrollment that is too low, but due to budgetary issues caused by larger student bodies growing faster than the college in question could support financially.

An interesting result of these factors is that starting around the year 2000, more and more colleges and universities across the United States began to accept both the SAT and the ACT for the first time. By 2010, every reputable college and university in the US had made clear to applicants that they accepted either of the two tests. There is still a regional bias to which students tend to take the SAT and which students tend to take the ACT.

Interestingly, I have noticed an unexpected trend in which students in New England, a long-standing bastion of the SAT, have chosen to either take both the SAT and ACT or solely the ACT. Recently, I have observed that the highest scoring students, those with the best grades in the toughest classes applying to the most competitive colleges, have explored the ACT to see if it provides a better result for applications. On the other hand, students who have struggled with the SAT have explored the ACT due to its reputation as a more straightforward, academic test than the tricky SAT.

In 2016, both the SAT and the ACT underwent another set of revisions, similar to those in 2005, the early 1990s, and countless more in the preceding decades. These latest revisions, more noticeably dramatic on the SAT, brought the two tests into a state of similarity never previously seen. The two tests are more similar in structure, format, and timing than ever before.

The current versions of the tests may look similar, but the philosophical differences between the two tests remain as stark as they did back in the late 1950s. With that in mind, we will explore how to create a test prep program for yourself or your school that covers either test, and possibly both, while supporting an individual college application process plan and/or a college counseling program.

Chapter 5
THE COLLEGE APPLICATION PROCESS

The primary focus of this book is setting up and fulfilling a test prep program, whether for an individual student (or for yourself) or for a class of students at either a school or an after-school program. Standardized tests like the SAT and the ACT are only one specific piece of the college application process. They have been blown out of proportion for most applicants, mostly due to the nature of taking a standardized test.

In juxtaposition to a high school student's grades, usually represented by a grade point average (GPA), which are built through taking and completing different semester- or year-long courses over several school years, the scores generated by the SAT or ACT occur due to the efforts of a single day.

The singularity of the experience of taking the SAT or the ACT lends an undeserved importance to SAT and ACT scores in the minds of students and parents, in addition to some educators. Guidance and college counselors know better and they do their best to communicate this to the students with whom they work.

Unfortunately, not all students can count on enough attention from their guidance or college counselors, usually despite the best efforts of those counselors. Budget cuts, shrinking departments, and increasing workloads have overwhelmed counseling departments at schools across the country, even at independent and charter schools.

Thankfully, I have had the good fortune to work with, know, and build friendships with both some of the most experienced guidance and college counselors I have ever met and college admissions officers who have served in that capacity at numerous colleges and universities around the nation. By picking their brains over the course of the last eighteen plus years, I have developed a strong understanding of how the college application process works.

I have shared what I have learned from friends and colleagues, happily, with their enthusiastic permission, at college fairs, at high school parent nights, and in our Livius tutoring centers. I have made videos for our YouTube channel on this topic and presented a podcast in which I discussed the process with knowledgeable guests. I am happy to share what I know and, hopefully, offset the stress produced by the college application process.

The college admission process begins well before most students even begin to think about the standardized tests taken during junior year of high school. The single most important factor in the admissions process is your grades, and grades begin to count in freshman year. It is true that some students take high school level classes in eighth grade, but that is a very tiny number, so the vast majority of students only need to worry about their actual grades beginning in ninth grade.

A high GPA is not merely built from the raw grades that students achieve in their classes. College admissions officers care just as much about how a student achieved their grades as they care about in what classes. Let's take a short tangent into the debate about weighted GPAs.

A grade point average is calculated by a school by comparing the grades a student earns with the number of credits a student can receive by passing classes. Most high schools award three or four credits for an academic class like history or math and one or two credits for a nonacademic class like gym or chorus. Grades are worth points, such that an A is four points, a B is three points, a C is two points, a D is one point, and an F is zero points.

For example, a student named Jane Example attends a school which awards four credits for each academic class and two for each nonacademic class. The grades in this example will be simplified to ignore any pluses or minuses to make this easier to understand. If Jane earns two As, two Bs, and a C in history, English, math, physics, and Spanish, respectively, and an A in chorus, you can calculate her GPA by adding up the number of points she earned per credit. Since she earned four points for the A in history, we can multiply those four points times the four credits for the class to get sixteen points. Her B in math results in multiplying three points times four credits to get twelve points. On the other hand, the A in chorus is only worth eight points, since the class is worth fewer credits. In total, Jane earned seventy-two points, which, when divided by the twenty-two credits' worth of classes she is taking, accounts for a GPA of 3.27.

Most high schools adjust the point values of grades for honors and Advanced Placement (AP) classes to account for the competitiveness of class rankings. The idea is that a student who earned straight As in the easiest classes should not rank higher than a student who challenged herself by taking honors or AP classes. The highest GPA a student who has only taken basic classes can earn is a 4.0. A student who is taking an honors class, however, has the opportunity to earn five points for an A, and some schools give an even greater weight to AP classes, allowing students to earn 5.5 points for an A in such a class.

Let's revisit our previous example. Let's pretend Jane has a sister named Joan. Joan is also taking history, English, math, physics, and Spanish, as well as chorus. Joan, however, has chosen to challenge herself by taking honors level in history, math, and English, and AP level in physics. Even if Joan earns the exact same grades in her respective classes that Jane earned, she would instead earn five points for her A in history, which, when we account for the four credits the class is worth, give Joan twenty points for history. Additionally, Joan would earn 4.5 points for her B in AP Physics at her school. Given those results, Joan would have a GPA of 4.09. This would guarantee that a student like Joan, who challenged herself by taking several honors classes and an AP class, would rank higher than another student who may have earned all As, but by taking lower-level, less challenging classes.

Technically, college admissions offices "unweight" these weighted GPAs during the admissions process. However, they account for these more challenging classes by awarding a value for each honors level course a student completes. Additionally, colleges will award an even higher value for each AP (or International Baccalaureate [IB]) course a student successfully completes. These values could, in fact, be point values. Many colleges and universities, especially public colleges, use a points system for each metric submitted by applicants to determine eligibility. Everything from quantitative metrics such as GPAs and test scores to qualitative metrics such as college application essays and portfolios receive a point value, which can then be measured to see if a student qualifies for admission. In terms of honors and AP/IB level classes, college admissions officers are looking to see that applicants challenged themselves academically while in high school.

Grades, in the form of the GPA and a raw number of honors and AP/IB classes, are the first things that college admissions officers consider in the application process. What those grades mean is the second factor. It is at this point that college admissions officers look at the circumstances surrounding those grades and how students accomplished them. This includes considering and, depending on the college, awarding points for the quality of the high school the student attended. Admissions officers look to see if a student excelled in a particularly prestigious or academically challenging school, such as an elite public high school, charter school, or independent high school. Achieving success in a highly competitive environment can attract the attention of an admissions officer.

Just as compelling, though, is the student who achieved high levels of success in an underresourced, economically depressed environment like an inner-city or rural public or parochial school. A student who earns a high GPA taking honors and AP classes in a school with little to no support has shown admissions officers a personal drive and strength of character that is very appealing. Additionally, students who come from economically depressed communities often have compelling stories about overcoming difficult circumstances coupled with the likelihood of coming from a more ethnically diverse background. Students like that can contribute to increasing the diversity of a historically homogenous campus into resembling something more similar to the actual demographics of the country as a whole.

In fact, students who attend schools in the middle of this paradigm, schools that are neither excellent nor struggling, are the ones who are at a disadvantage in this equation. With neither a compelling story of overcoming numerous obstacles nor the opportunities offered by a highly prestigious or rigorous educational environment, students from schools that fall in the middle can seem bland by comparison.

Only once the factors surrounding a student's GPA and how that student achieved those grades are considered do college admissions officers look at standardized test scores. One of the interesting things about how college admissions officers consider test scores is that there is generally not a threshold over which good scores exist and under which bad scores exist. Instead, admissions officers tend to look at scores as a spectrum. As an outside observer, you can actually see this spectrum in the numbers colleges and universities are required to report publicly.

Every college is required to publicly release the scores of the students they have accepted the previous year. Since colleges and universities tend to accept thousands of students, it is unwieldy for them to list out the anonymized score of all of the students they accept. Instead, colleges release this information as a range of scores, usually both on their own websites and to college counseling websites, such as the College Board's BigFuture page.

Let's look at the University of California at Los Angeles (UCLA) and examine the score range for the students admitted for the fall of 2016 and fall of 2017, the most recent data available at the time this book was written. Of the over 113,000 high school graduates who applied to UCLA for admission for the fall of 2016, just under 16,000 earned admission, an acceptance rate of approximately 14 percent, making UCLA a highly selective college. While only 6,200 of those 16,000 students accepted to UCLA matriculated into the school for freshman year, the SAT score range applies to all of the admitted students, even if they didn't end up attending UCLA. The score ranges on the SAT for students admitted to UCLA in 2016 and 2017 were 640–740 in (evidence-based reading and writing) English and 630–780 in math. Overall, the total SAT score range was 1,270–1,520. Other than these numbers looking very good, what does any of this actually mean?

Let's do a thought experiment. Imagine a college only accepts one hundred freshmen, and all of the accepted students decide to matriculate and attend that college. Now, imagine the students arrive on campus to attend freshman orientation. At orientation, the school's staff decides to line up all of the new students based on their SAT scores. Of course, this would never happen. Not only would the freshman orientation staff at a college never do such a thing, but the truth is that SAT and ACT scores no longer have meaning once you are accepted to and go to college. No one cares about SAT or ACT scores anymore after you've started college.

Back to the thought experiment. For the purposes of this experiment, let's pretend that our imaginary college has the same score ranges as UCLA. Once all of the students are lined up from lowest SAT English score to highest SAT English score, the student in the twenty-fifth spot in the line will have a score of 640 and the student in the seventy-fifth spot in the line will have a score of 740. All of the students in the line in between the twenty-fifth and seventy-fifth spots will have scores in increasing numerical order between 640 and 740. That is what a score range is: it shows the twenty-fifth and seventy-fifth percentile scores for that population.

So, the middle 50 percent of students accepted to UCLA in 2016 and 2017 had SAT English scores between 640 and 740, generally a high range of results. The interesting thing about these 25/75 score ranges is that they tell us that approximately 25 percent of students accepted to UCLA during this period scored lower than 640 on the SAT English. Whether the students who scored lower than 640 on the SAT English section and earned admission to UCLA had GPAs that were outstanding or had other factors that helped them secure admission was most likely determined on a case-by-case basis.

Clearly, there is no single score on the SAT English section a student must achieve in order to qualify for admissions. The same is true for SAT math scores and total SAT scores. On the other hand, students who score at or above the top of the score range may have a better chance to earn admission, especially combined with a strong GPA. At the very least, students with a combination of high test scores and strong GPAs will have cleared the first hurdle in the admissions process.

Despite the fact that students can earn admission to a school with an SAT or ACT score below the twenty-fifth percentile, many parents are concerned about a student submitting low test scores, even when a student has, in fact, achieved a result that is within the middle or upper range. Luckily, there is something called "superscoring." Superscoring means that a college considers all of the SAT or ACT scores that a student submits, but only utilizes the best results in their admissions process.

Imagine you took the SAT twice, scoring a 600 in English and a 650 in math, for a total score of 1,250. If you are applying to UCLA, you might feel that you want to take the SAT again to increase your numbers to something that is more helpful, especially considering that the English score is below the twenty-fifth percentile as well. On the second SAT, after extensively practicing your English skills, you score a 700 on English, but your math score goes down to 600, for a total SAT result of 1,300. Despite the improvement in English, you might feel disappointed. The good news is that UCLA, like almost all colleges in the US, will use your 700 in English from the second SAT and the 650 in math from the first SAT, and count them as a superscore of 1,350, better than you achieved on an individual SAT.

Once a college admissions officer determines that a student is academically qualified for that school, the real work begins. Even with a public focus on numbers like GPAs and SAT scores, most colleges take numerous other factors into consideration during the college application process that have nothing to do with numbers. In fact, a data-driven approach to college admissions is actually a relatively recent development. In the period before the 1890s, the majority of students were accepted either due to family connections or letters of recommendation from luminaries within a candidate's life, such as a local politician or religious leader.

Even today, letters of recommendation carry a certain amount of weight in the admissions process. It is at this point that admissions officers look at the recommendations submitted by students. Most colleges require a letter from a guidance or college counselor, which is usually a perfunctory form letter, and one letter from a teacher chosen by the student. If a student is lucky, a college will allow the submission of additional letters of recommendation. The more information a student can provide is always better.

Especially in situations in which a college does not accept additional letters, choosing the right teacher to write a letter of recommendation is essential. Most students with whom I have spoken tend toward selecting a teacher who awarded high grades to the student. Instead, I often recommend that students ask a teacher, regardless of how the student did in their class(es) with this teacher, with whom they have a long-standing and strong relationship. A teacher who is also a club advisor, coach, or academic advisor is often a powerful choice to write a letter of recommendation.

Most colleges and universities require students to submit a résumé in addition to listing classes, extracurricular activities, and work experience directly in the application. What a student has chosen to do with her time is an important factor in learning who that student is, so far as college admissions officers are concerned.

There was a period in the late 1980s through the 2000s in which the concept of the "well-rounded student" was popular. The idea was that a student who had a variety of experiences in her background was a better candidate because she would be more likely to participate in a variety of experiences on campus. Theoretically, such a candidate could call upon her varied experiences to better connect with a diverse campus community. Unfortunately, this did not prove to be true. Instead, candidates who show focus and dedication to a handful of activities are more likely to contribute to the community on campus, especially if they have shown a penchant for taking leadership roles in high school. Focus and dedication mean not merely participating in a sport, club, or activity, but diving deep and demonstrating true passion.

In other words, the student who joins a hundred clubs in high school may get his picture in the yearbook a hundred times, but he has showed colleges that he wasn't that interested in any one thing. The student who focuses on a few specific activities, like one or two sports, one or two clubs, or different positions in the performing arts, and then dedicates the time to reach a high level of achievement, including leadership positions, will be more likely to do the same at the college level.

In fact, students who have an overwhelmingly strong focus in one area tend to stand out. Colleges do not expect their star athletes to join a hundred clubs. They expect the star athlete to excel in his sport.

Similarly, colleges expect the lead chair oboist to excel at the oboe in the college orchestra. That athlete or oboist may join a club or two in a secondary area of interest, such as the science fiction and comic book clubs or a sorority or a cultural organization, perhaps even two of those, but focus and dedication to a few things is more important than wandering around campus not truly participating in anything.

To utilize Harvard as an example again, we already know that Harvard will receive approximately forty thousand applications each year and will only be able to accommodate approximately two thousand freshmen. The mistake is thinking of those two thousand freshmen as a single pool of candidates. Instead, it is better to think of them as a series of different constituencies, some larger and some smaller. Remember our oboist in the school orchestra? One day she will graduate from Harvard and go out into the world. Now the director of the Harvard orchestra needs a new oboist. How many students applying to Harvard pay the oboe? Five? Ten? Thirteen? So, it is not forty thousand applicants vying for that one freshman spot, it is five or ten or thirteen candidates. It is even likely that all of the oboe candidates will have the grades and test scores to qualify for admission to Harvard, but only one will likely make it. No one else matters for that spot.

Given the number of high schools in the United States, both public and private, there are far more valedictorians graduating every school year than there are freshman spots at all eight Ivy League colleges. Therefore, even though most colleges never mention a word about how many valedictorians they accept or reject, it is likely that many schools turn down more valedictorians than they accept. Why then would one high-grade/high-scoring candidate earn acceptance while another is rejected? At that level, it becomes about something more than just grades. Focus on and dedication to something that can contribute to campus life beyond just academics is one answer. Personal narrative is the other.

The last major factor in a college application is the essay. Because the essay is seen as the final step in the process, many students, parents, and educators make the mistake of thinking it is the least important. I believe, however, that as the final step in the process, it is the most important. By the time a candidate has submitted transcripts which highlight good grades in rigorous courses; score reports full of top SAT, ACT, and SAT subject test scores; letters of recommendation introducing the student's environment and how she fits into it; and a full application along with a résumé that lists and explains all of the student's activities, jobs, awards, and achievements, she has provided enough information to overcome several hurdles in the process. Now it is the time to help the admissions get to know the candidate. The college application essay does that.

There are two other factors in the college application process that are not currently universal: the interview and the portfolio. For a long time, an interview was an integral part of the college application process. This was because most college students attended a college in their home state for most of American history, dating back to colonial times. The same paradigm shift that saw the number and percentage of high school graduates applying to and attending college skyrocket beginning in the 1990s also saw more and more students apply to, achieve acceptance to, and attend colleges out of state. One interesting artifact of this shift was that more and more students applied to colleges that they did not have a chance to visit, meaning there was little to no opportunity to sit for an interview.

The period between the early 1990s and the 2010s saw the number of colleges and universities requiring interviews plummet. Some colleges responded by increasing the opportunities for alumni interviews and the number of high school tours held by admissions staff. Interestingly, with so many students applying to college now, an interview is a great way for the admissions officers to get to know candidates better. As such, I strongly recommend booking an interview with a touring admissions officer if you do not have the chance to visit campus. Alumni interviews are also helpful. Make sure you practice your conversation skills and have answers to common questions in mind before you meet with a representative from your top-choice college.

Portfolios, once only the province of art school candidates, are becoming more common in applications to colleges and universities of all kinds. A portfolio historically included examples of artworks, whether fine arts, music, theatre, or film, created by students to help art school admissions officers gauge the qualifications of an art school candidate in the way a transcript would do the same for a purely academic candidate. Many students are finding, however, that a portfolio of work created in fields other than the arts can further lay the groundwork to help admissions officers understand the background and circumstances of candidacy better.

Modern non-arts portfolios can include examples of scientific experiments and science fair entries by STEM students; business plans and the results of completed projects by young entrepreneurs; or a collection of articles and media highlighting the successes of athletes, social volunteers, and high school campus leaders. A portfolio can be a paper-based document, audio files, or a video reel. Two factors are essential in creating a portfolio. First, confirm that a college will accept your portfolio before submitting it. Second, professionalism and intent are the primary factors in creating a portfolio that succeeds in telling the narrative you want to tell. Make choices and then follow through on them. Don't cobble something together and tell yourself the lie that it is good enough. Focus and dedication apply to a portfolio as well as the application and résumé.

One final factor is considered by some colleges and universities, some of the time: financial considerations. Most colleges and universities are "need blind," meaning they do not consider a candidate's ability to pay for college in the admissions process. This is to prevent bias against students from depressed socioeconomic backgrounds or for students from wealthy, privileged backgrounds. Some schools do consider the ability to pay in the admissions process for two very specific reasons, one to the student's benefit and one against. The first, beneficial, consideration is that some schools are specifically looking to attract or recruit students from less privileged and even depressed socioeconomic backgrounds both as a method for increasing diversity on campus and because they have a certain amount of money they are required to spend on financial aid per endowments and grants. The second, less beneficial, consideration is that some colleges have limitations on their ability to support need-based scholarships and can only accept a certain number of students who have high levels of financial need.

Once a student has submitted all of the required parts of the application, along with transcripts, recommendations, score reports, the essay and supplemental writing samples, and portfolio, if allowed, the application is out of the student's hands. Now it is up to the admissions officer. Since there are currently approximately 4,300 colleges and universities in the United States, it is safe to say that each college has its own process. In general, though, all colleges tend to follow similar paths to determining which candidates are accepted and rejected.

Most colleges assign each individual admissions officer a region of the United States and that officer receives and reviews all of the applications from candidates who live in the region. Many colleges have a dedicated foreign applicant admissions officer, while many others distribute foreign candidates among their staff. Some colleges have admissions officers who focus on certain populations not limited by geography such as minority candidates or applicants to specialty schools or departments on campus like arts or honors programs.

Regardless of how a college divvies up the pool of candidates among the admissions officers, each individual officer reads through thousands of applications during the application season. From that impossibly large pool of candidates, each admissions officer finds several hundred or more applications which have piqued her attention. And from amongst those, she has picked out her favored candidates, those for whom she will fight to offer them admission.

While it may appear at this point that only one person has absolute power over each application, that isn't exactly true. Many schools employ a large team of part-time application readers to presort applications based on dozens of different factors. These prereaders will often pull aside applications from candidates who are clearly not academically qualified for the college in question, although each of those application will still get a second read just in case extenuating circumstances interest an admissions officer in that candidacy. Even then, most applications will receive an additional read by a second admissions officer, who will make his own recommendation as to the viability of that candidacy.

Once the application deadlines have passed and the initial reads are complete, the admissions officers assemble in a conference room and the real action begins. Admissions officers will present their favored candidates and debate their applications and requirements. Even candidates that admissions officers don't favor get their time at the table, just in case another admissions officer wants to review an application. For each applicant, the team votes on the candidacy. In the likely event that they have either too many or too few acceptances at the conclusion of this process, they start over with the candidates who were on the bubble, as the sports metaphor goes, and give them a second round.

More than just looking for two thousand qualified candidates, such as the number of freshmen who are accepted by Harvard each year, admissions officers are looking for students who not only meet the academic qualifications of the institution but fill a niche in the greater community on campus. While colleges and universities were rather homogenous before the 1960s, the majority of colleges and universities today look for a diverse community on campus that more accurately reflects the various demographic diversities of the United States as a whole.

In other words, admissions officers are looking to accept high-flying, high-scoring academic students, but not just that. They want students who hail from a wide variety of ethnic and racial backgrounds; students whose interests cover athletics, the arts, social justice, community service, and popular culture; and students whose efforts will not be limited to the classroom, but all aspects of life on campus.

Then, at the end of the process, the admissions team has the list of students who will be accepted for the following school year. The list often contains more names than there are freshman spots, however. To use the example of UCLA again, in 2017 the school accepted over 16,000 candidates, but only approximately 6,200 students enrolled for the following fall. That means that almost 10,000 candidates were accepted to UCLA but chose to attend school elsewhere. This is true at every college and university. Harvard accepts approximately

2,000 students each year, but there are only 1,600 freshmen enrolled each fall.

This is because most students apply to an average of seven to ten colleges, with that average rising steadily since the late 1980s. A quick glance at social media sites such as YouTube and Twitter will unearth videos and posts by high school students who have applied to ten, fifteen, or even twenty colleges and universities. Guidance and college counselors advise students to apply to a wide selection of schools that include one or more "reach" schools, one or more "safety" schools, and a healthy pool of "target" schools. Ultimately, though, a student can only attend one college or university, regardless of how many applications she sends out. That means that all of the other schools who accept that student will get rejected in turn.

College admissions teams know this is going to happen, which explains why they accept more students than the college can accommodate freshman year. Decades of institutional experience has taught the team approximately what number of acceptances will lead to the correct number of enrollments. This is not an exact science, though. Sometimes, more accepted students will enroll than the admissions office anticipated, which can lead to more freshmen seeking on-campus housing than there are beds. Many a student has a story of an unnatural triple, myself included.

On the other hand, fewer accepted students can enroll than expected, which leads to the admissions team dipping into the list of students who were waitlisted. The waitlist is the purgatory where students go when they clearly have the academic qualifications to earn acceptance to a college, but did not quite make the cut, usually due to a judgment call based on factors outside the applicant's control, such as too many students with enticing personal narratives in that year's applicant pool. In my opinion, the waitlist is equivalent to a college saying no, but with love. Students on the waitlist do get accepted from time to time, but not often enough for me to suggest anything other than "Move on" to students who have been placed into the middle ground of the waitlist.

Ultimately, the goal of the process is to build an application packet that not only places your qualifications in the best light, but fully introduces you to the college admissions officers who read your application. I often tell students that you want to invite the admissions officers to fall in love with the idea of you. You want an admissions officer to happily imagine bumping into you on campus over the next four years. You want to inspire an admissions officer to stand up and fight for you in a crowded, hot, smelly conference room and to not give in until the other admissions officers yield and vote you in.

Chapter 6
WILL THE SAT AND ACT REMAIN RELEVANT?

When the University of Chicago announced in June 2018 that the school was going "test optional," the internet exploded with commentary predicting the quick and awful slide of the SAT and ACT into obscurity. Then, the University of Chicago announced that over 98 percent of applicants for the admission to the class of 2023, the freshmen enrolling in the fall of 2019, submitted ACT or SAT scores as part of their application packets. So, which is it? Are standardized tests doomed to slide into the dustbin of history, or are the SAT and ACT here to stay? The answer is likely both.

In the short term, the SAT and the ACT are still very relevant to the college application process. Even though the test-optional movement is growing, every college and university in the country, except Hampshire College in Massachusetts, a school founded as an alternative model college, accepts test scores, even if a school in question doesn't require test scores.

The term *test optional* means that a college will evaluate an application from a candidate that does not include the submission of standardized test scores without any bias against that candidate. Schools who accept applications that do not include test scores may require students who submit test-optional applications to write an additional essay, submit a portfolio, and provide additional information to fill the hole in the application left by not submitting test scores.

The test-optional movement actually began in the late 1960s, just as the SAT and ACT had finally gained universal acceptance by colleges as the admissions exam of choice. By this time, the entrance exams that the majority of colleges had produced and used in their individual application processes had been laid aside in favor of either the SAT or ACT. In 1969, however, Bowdoin College in Maine became the first college to go test optional. Even considering that fifty-year history of accepting applications without test scores, Bowdoin has stated on its website that approximately 70 percent of applicants vying for admission for the fall of 2019 still submitted scores.

While the number of schools who declare themselves test optional will likely continue to grow, it is also likely that the number and percentage of students applying to colleges who continue to submit scores will remain relatively constant. Since students are often taking the SAT or ACT or both anyway as part of the process of applying to schools that are not test optional, they often submit scores to test-optional colleges as a matter of course. Even with the growth of the test-optional movement, the majority of four-year colleges and universities still require standardized test scores, especially public universities that are required to submit reams of data to the state legislatures which fund them.

This is true even for the University of California (UC) colleges. The Board of Governors of the UC system voted to suspend the use of the SAT or ACT in admissions decisions through 2023 due to the cancellation of the March, May, and June 2020 SAT test dates and the April 2020 ACT test date over concerns about social distancing and stay-in-place orders during the coronavirus pandemic crisis. Even so, it is likely the admissions offices of the various UC colleges will either reinstate the SAT and ACT as admissions requirements in 2023, if not sooner, or be forced to find another standardized test to use in the admissions process.

Colleges and universities that require test scores do so because the administration and admissions teams at those schools believe that the SAT and the ACT provide valuable information on applicants. The conceits that the SAT can be used as an intelligence test or that the SAT or ACT can predict college success have long since been disproven. The SAT and the ACT do provide some information to colleges on candidates' problem-solving and analytical reading abilities, which colleges extrapolate to mean that students with both high test scores and good grades are more likely to maintain a strong academic record going forward.

So long as colleges and universities believe that they accrue valuable information about students from SAT or ACT scores, they will continue to accept these scores in the admission process. Additionally, colleges and universities use SAT and ACT scores in both course placement and in financial aid decision-making. Many colleges partially determine merit-based scholarship awards on PSAT, SAT, and ACT results. Podcaster and technology pundit John Gruber often tells a story of his own college application process in the early 1990s in which he was offered a full scholarship to Drexel University based on his high SAT scores in order to lure him away from matriculating at other, potentially more prestigious, colleges.

In order for colleges and universities to abandon the use of the SAT or the ACT in the college application process, they would require some other tool on which they could depend for all the information and purposes they use the SAT or ACT. Other organizations have worked to develop tests that colleges can use in place of the SAT or ACT in the college application process, for determining course placement, and for awarding merit-based scholarships, but even computer-based tests would run into the same quandary as the SAT or ACT. Some students struggle with standardized testing while many, many more have the potential to do well, but lack the resources to practice and improve their skills.

The only way colleges and universities completely abandon standardized tests is if a new paradigm arises in the same way the multiple-choice test, first invented in the 1910s, replaced the text-based entrance exams introduced in the nineteenth century. Like most social and technological shifts, it is difficult to predict what will happen until the change is upon us. So, is it possible that colleges and universities will abandon the SAT or ACT? Yes, but not until something better comes along. Until then, the SAT and the ACT are still relevant in the college application process.

Chapter 7
THE SCIENCE OF TUTORING FOR PARENTS

WHAT DID THE 2019 COLLEGE ADMISSIONS CHEATING SCANDAL TEACH US?

T he story broke with a splash across the spectrum of news outlets from serious journalistic organizations to entertainment magazines and gossip websites. A collection of superwealthy parents had been indicted on dozens of charges after the ringleader of the scam, William Rick Singer, had pled guilty to bribing college sports coaches and other officials and coordinating a scheme to help certain students cheat on the SAT and ACT. Beloved actors such as Felicity Huffman, Academy Award–nominated star of *Desperate Housewives*, and Lori Laughlin, Aunt Becky on the perennially popular *Full House* and its sequel *Fuller House*, were indicted along with bankers, CEOs, and fashion designer Mossimo.

The scandal focused on two types of fraud. Some parents were engaged in the direct bribery of coaches and college officials through a fake charitable organization run by Singer. The coaches would then lie to their own college's admissions offices about the athletic prowess of the students. Students with absolutely no experience in sports, such as tennis, sailing, soccer, water polo, or volleyball, were offered admission based on the request of the coach. The student would participate peripherally in the athletic program during freshman year, some going so far as to sit on the bench during games, and then get cut from the team before sophomore year. Since the students were not on athletic scholarships and the parents were paying full tuition due to their wealth, the students were able to continue at the school with no questions asked by the college administrations.

The other type of fraud involved cheating on the standardized tests, including the SAT and the ACT. Singer and his team at his college "counseling" company would first bribe psychologists to draft letters outlining unique combinations of learning disabilities backdated to provide a history of need for accommodations. Once the College Board and ACT awarded the students accommodations, he told the parents to request an alternate testing site far from home, usually due to the excuse of a family vacation. Singer bribed accommodation proctors at testing sites in West Hollywood, California, and Houston, Texas, and possibly others, which would then be selected by the parents as their vacation destinations. The students took the SAT or ACT under the watchful eyes of the bribed proctors. Apparently, some of the students were involved in the cheating, working with the bribed proctors to artificially inflate their scores, while other students were unaware of the bribery and cheating undertaken by their parents. The answer sheets for these students were altered after the fact.

In other cases, a man named Mark Riddell, who worked for Singer, took the exams on behalf of the students.

The scheme fell apart when one of the parents was indicted on unrelated charges. He flipped on both the Yale soccer coach, whom he was in the process of bribing, as well as Singer, who then flipped on the parents in an effort to reduce his own sentence upon pleading guilty. Since then, thirty-three parents have been indicted, over half of whom have pled guilty, including Laughlin and her husband. Numerous college coaches were fired, while some received indictments of their own. Colleges began to rescind offers of admission within weeks, followed by expulsions of students involved shortly thereafter.

The question that begs to be asked is why did the parents do it? Why did the parents invest tens if not hundreds of thousands of dollars in a scheme to bribe officials and cheat on standardized tests so their children could go to a specific school? The answer lies in the prestige of the institutions targeted by Singer and the parents. Regardless of the suitability of the colleges in question for the students involved, the parents seemed most interested in the names of the colleges rather than the educations afforded by these schools.

Some people seem to care only about the fame of the name of the school rather than what the student will experience on campus. No thought was put into whether the University of Southern California (USC) or Yale or Stanford was the best-fit college for those students. The name was the game. Too often students and parents place too much importance on the name of the school. Yes, writing the name Harvard or Georgetown on a résumé can cause a hiring manager to pause and take a second glance at an application, but that is still not a guarantee of anything.

More than just not trusting their own children to earn admission to the schools they preferred, the parents demonstrated a lack of trust in the entire system of college admissions. These parents used their wealth to unbalance the scales and essentially steal a spot at their chosen schools because they misunderstood the fundamental changes that have occurred in college admissions.

As we saw in chapter 4, prior to the advent of admissions testing beginning in the 1890s, fewer than 5 percent of all Americans attended college, and the majority of people who did came from the most privileged status of American society. There are stories of exceptional students from lower socioeconomic communities earning admission to a college or university during this period, but, for the most part, college was for the wealthy only. By the 1920s, so many students of limited means were passing entrance exams and earning admission to prestigious institutions that the privileged community who had been the historical beneficiaries of a college education added additional barriers to achieving a college degree from a prestigious institution for the average American. The 1920s saw the rise of community colleges, the expansion of public universities, and the growth of both women's colleges and historically black colleges and universities in response to the Ivy League schools, and similar institutions, imposing quota systems on poorer students and bans on women and African American students.

These barriers began to crumble in the 1960s due to multiple factors. The passage of the GI Bill and the baby boom led a large growth in the raw number of Americans applying to and attending college during the 1960s. Larger social movements, such as the civil rights movement, women's liberation movement, and anti-war movement, led to more students seeking out stronger educational programs, which were then forced to desegregate and go coeducational. And decades of the transition of the United States from a more agrarian society to a highly technological society led to an ever-increasing need for a more highly educated workforce.

As discussed in chapter 5, so many students are graduating high school and applying to college that individual schools can afford to be more selective than ever. In fact, colleges and universities no longer offer admissions to qualified students, but instead select a freshman class from among an unfathomably large pool of qualified candidates.

The population that was the entirety of the college student population as late as the 1890s, the sons of the incredibly wealthy, are now a tiny subpopulation within a college's student body: the legacy student. There is a persistent myth that legacy students (both male and female after the 1960s) take up huge portions of the freshman class at Ivy League schools and other prestigious colleges. Instead, the vast majority of students accepted to prestigious colleges and universities are not only the first generation of their families to attend that school, but are frequently the first generation of their families to attend college at all.

The admissions scandal parents misread the modern college admissions landscape badly. Harvard, Yale, Stanford, USC, and other prestigious colleges and universities look for more than merely grades and scores now. These schools use grades and scores as the first cutoff into the process. After that, they are looking for students who have a clear and interesting narrative. More importantly, all of the other colleges and universities in the country have been getting better and better over the last few decades as Ivy League–quality students have been denied admission to Ivy League schools overwhelmed with qualified applicants.

Instead, these excellent students have been accepted to colleges in the next tier or two down in historical prestige. The colleges and universities in those next tiers have also benefited from the growth in the number of highly educated graduates produced during the post-1960s and post-1993 periods, which has led to better quality professors at schools of all levels.

In fact, the quality of a college education has never been better. Every school from your local community college to the large public university to the selective private college has seen highly qualified professors spread out throughout all levels. A student graduating high school today can get an excellent education at almost any college in America.

What Ivy League colleges and their equivalents around the country offer today is the prestige of the name and an endowment that can afford both more money in need-based financial aid and on-campus resources. Other than that, the quality of the education is mostly the same around the country at colleges and universities of all levels.

Since the name of the school only provides a small benefit and the quality of education is approximately the same at all colleges, what makes the difference? Fit. Fit means finding the right environment for the personality, goals, and social needs of the student. That's what the admissions scandal parents ignored.

Imagine two universities that are located seven miles from each other in the Boston suburbs. They both rank in the mid- to low thirties each year in the U.S. News & World Report's top fifty national universities list, usually placed adjacent to each other. They offer similar majors and degree programs, have similar acceptance rates, and boast highly respected faculty. The GPAs and SAT scores of accepted applicants are almost identical. The lists of most popular clubs and activities on campus are nearly identical. At first glance, almost every-thing about these two universities is so similar as to seem identical.

One of these universities is Boston College, a medium-sized, pri-vate university founded by members of the Jesuit leadership in Boston in the mid-nineteenth century. Both the faculty and student body are predominantly Catholic to this day. The other of these universi-ties is Brandeis University, a medium-sized, private, secular university founded by Jewish social, political, and educational leaders shortly after World War II. Although the college is officially secular, the majority of both the faculty and student body are predominantly Jewish to this day.

Both of these colleges are excellent institutions, boasting award-winning faculty, illustrious alumni, and large, impressive campuses. A dedicated student could be successful at either institution. The differ-ence is fit.

Rather than focus on the name and accompanying prestige of a col-lege, the most important factor in selecting a college that will afford a student the best chance of a successful collegiate experience is the fit. Fit can mean culture or community. It can mean location. It can mean the programs and degrees offered by an institution. It can mean the depth and breadth of extracurricular activities available on campus. It usually means all of these and more.

In my opinion, these parents wasted their money. The college sports coaches burned their careers to the ground for no good reason. None of the adults in the admissions scandal did any favors to the students, especially those who were unaware of the multiple frauds perpetrated in their names. No adult took into consideration the best fit for the students. They thought only of themselves and the prestige that would flow onto them from their children attending a college with a famous name.

THE PARENT'S ROLE

Since it is clear that participating in a national scheme to bribe officials and cheat on standardized tests to defraud the admissions offices of prestigious universities is not the correct way to help your children attain admission to college, what is the proper role for a parent in the college admissions process?

Parents have long struggled with how best to help their children through the college application process, especially considering all the changes that occur between generations. The college application process that current grandparents experienced in the 1940s and 1950s was radically different from the process their children, today's parents, experienced in the 1970s, 1980s, and 1990s, just as that experience was radically different form the experience today's high school graduates are navigating today. Yesterday's good advice often does not provide any help today.

Parents often find themselves falling into three broad generalizations during their own children's college application process: the helicopter parent, the eager but confused parent, and the laissez-faire parent. Interestingly, I have observed the same parent, or pair of parents, fill each of these three roles at different times with each of their different children.

The helicopter parent hovers over the student, adjusting, critiquing, and advising at every opportunity. No step in the process is complete without a contribution from the helicopter parent. The helicopter parent is comfortable hiring tutors or private college counselors, especially early in the process, but inserts opinions and suggestions at every turn. The helicopter parent has been known to take a strong hand in editing application essays, participate in filling out applications, and selecting colleges for the college list.

The confused but eager parent wants to help but doesn't know how. Even though this parent may have gone to college back in the day, their own process was so long ago that they don't remember the details. They are not sure how to proceed and often procrastinate on important steps in the application process in the hope that the student will take a more active role. Eventually, the confused but eager parent turns to tutors and private college counselors at the last minute, desperate for someone to save the day.

The laissez-faire parent makes it clear to the student from the beginning that the student is responsible for their own college application process. This parent usually sets expectations and then divorces themselves from the process. Unexpectedly, this parent has no trouble hiring a tutor or private college counselor to guide the student but expects the student to handle everything about the process, including scheduling, deadlines, and all communication with colleges, teachers, tutors, and counselors once the bill has been paid.

If you find yourself falling into one of these three categories, don't despair, as each archetype can teach us something useful about the best practices for guiding a student through the college application process. Generally, a more balanced approach is a more collaborative and successful approach.

The helicopter parent teaches us that the parent has to be directly involved in the process. High school students, even those who are eighteen years old and legally adults, are still children at heart. The college application process is a complicated, multistep experience and can be daunting even to the most academically motivated student. Parent involvement is essential to a successful conclusion to the process.

The helicopter parent also teaches us the value of boundaries. While every high school student applying to college needs parental guidance, ultimately the student needs to do this on their own. The student must be the person to write the college application essay. The student must be the person to fill out the applications. The student must take responsibility for their own process. While the parent can guide, the student is the one who must do.

The confused but eager parent reminds us that this is a complicated and confusing process. Don't be afraid to admit you don't have all the answers. Even if a student chooses to apply to the exact same college as her parents, and that is the student's top-choice college, enough time has passed that the process will be completely different. Admitting and accepting that you are confused opens you up to learning about the college application process as it currently stands.

The confused but eager parent also reminds us that procrastination is the worst possible solution to any problem. Time may be an obstacle, but it is also an opportunity. Parents and students who start the process earlier can often get more attention from tutors, teachers, school guidance counselors, private college counselors, and college admissions officers due to the seasonal and cyclical nature of the school year and college application season. There are times of the year when education professionals are less busy and starting early gives parents and students the chance to get the help they need to be more calm, comfortable, and successful in this process. More importantly, don't be afraid to ask for help. The teachers and counselors at your school want to help. Private tutors and college counselors are there to help. College admissions officers are eager to help. Asking for help also provides a good model for students about to go off to college by themselves.

The laissez-faire parent teaches us that the student is the primary stakeholder in her own college application process. It is the student who must take primary responsibility for following all the steps and completing the application. However much a parent may want to rescue their child because they recognize the importance of a good college education and that a positive college experience can lead to a joyful future, it is the student's life and it is the student's path to follow. The student must be the one who walks that path.

The laissez-faire parent also teaches us that placing the onus of responsibility on the student does not mean abandoning the student to her own devices. No teenager is either experienced enough or mature enough to be completely self-motivated. Nor are they knowledgeable enough about the world to know everything they need for the application process. An adult perspective is essential to guide a student successfully. While teachers, guidance counselors, tutors, and private college counselors can be incredibly helpful through this process, there is no substitute for parental involvement. While we agree that helicoptering in is not the answer, participation is required.

Things to Do

As the parent, you are the student's guide. Imagine yourself leading a tour through Disney World, or a comparable theme park. Everyone enters through the same entrance, but there are numerous paths through the park, and the combinations of the order in which you can experience the rides are infinite. Your job is not to grab the student's hand and force them along a particular path or towards a particular experience, but to highlight the options available and to support the student through the journey.

The first step in any successful endeavor is creating a plan. Spontaneity and improvisation are positive things, since life rarely goes exactly according to plan; however, having a plan opens the door to spontaneity and improvisation. The opposite of having a plan is actually procrastination. At the end of this chapter, you will find a timeline graphic, which you can use to create a plan for a testing calendar. Fortunately, standardized tests like the SAT and the ACT are only one small part of the college application process.

Set deadlines for researching and building a college list. The college list is often the most contentious part of the partnership between parents and students. Students and parents often have different expectations and goals when selecting colleges for the initial college list. The thing to remember is that there are no bad choices at the beginning of the process. Even though a student may only end up applying to a small handful of colleges, or as many as ten or more, the initial college list is actually a list of colleges to research. A first draft of a college list may include as many colleges as you like. In fact, the more colleges on the initial list, the better.

Keep an open mind about colleges. There are over 4,300 colleges and universities in the United States alone, and I guarantee there are many excellent colleges that are new to you. When I first attended graduate school, I made a new friend, who is, to this day, one of the closest friends I have. He, his wife, and their housemate all attended Carleton College in Minnesota. I am from New Jersey originally, and I had never heard of Carleton College despite conducting what I thought was an extensive college search process during high school. That was my mistake. Carleton has historically ranked in the U.S. News & World Report's top five national liberal arts colleges. Just because I hadn't heard of Carleton, that did not negate the excellence of the college.

Additionally, be open to what your student wants to study, even if that includes art. Many parents are concerned that if a student chooses a major with no seemingly practical job prospects, that student could be doomed to a life of poverty. Before you hit the panic button, keep a few things in mind. First, majoring in an art does not guarantee a life of poverty. Look around the room in which you are reading this book. Every item in that room was designed by someone, and that someone likely has an art degree. More importantly, numerous studies have shown that the average college student changes majors at least twice in their college career. College is about exploring different ideas and concepts in a relatively low-consequence environment. If you are worried that your student is setting herself up for failure due to interest in a particular major, you are probably overthinking the situation. There are jobs out there for everyone.

Once the student has built an initial college list, start to plan college visits. In fact, you and your child can start to visit colleges even before the two of you have built that first college list. Most colleges and universities offer on-campus programs open to the local community, even beyond sporting events, and this experience can make young students more comfortable when visiting college campuses during the application process.

Visiting colleges far from home can be time consuming and expensive, so consider visiting comparable colleges and universities closer to home. Imagine a family that lives in the western part of North Carolina. In this family there is a student who wishes to apply to Harvard University; however, the family doesn't have the wherewithal to fly or drive up to Boston to visit Harvard. Instead, the family should consider visiting Duke University, which could be approximately a four- to five-hour drive away, even if Duke is not on that student's college list. Since Duke is also a top-ranked private national research university, it can provide a comparable tour experience to a student interested in a college like Harvard or Yale in the Northeast, Stanford in California, Rice University in Texas, or the University of Chicago in the Midwest. More importantly, there are colleges of comparable prestige and demographics throughout the country.

Another important task that a parent can accomplish to help a student through the application process is to collect and organize financial information. The vast majority of high-school-aged students have no concept of their parents' financial situation. For both financial aid applications and for consideration by need-aware colleges, this information is essential to the process. This is one area in which parents should take the lead, since students will rarely have access to this information.

Lastly, remove obstacles to the student completing tasks on their own. Help your student clear a study space, which can improve grades in school and results on standardized tests. Help your student with a calendar or other schedule system so they can finish tasks, keep track of work schedules, and still have time for downtime and sleep. Most importantly, help your student stay positive through this process by rewarding successful completion of tasks, even if only with kind words and a smile. Positive reinforcement can be a powerful motivator to a student.

Things to Try

With so many changes to the college application process since current parents were students themselves, the amount of information available can be overwhelming. Even though most parents are finished with school by the time their own children are applying to college, the time for learning is never over. Take the opportunity to participate in parent nights and college fairs whenever they occur.

Most high schools hold parent nights several times throughout the school year. A parent night is a great time to meet your student's current teachers and to catch up with teachers from previous years. Students are usually welcome at parent nights, and they represent a unique chance for students to renew and strengthen relationships with teachers who might end up as perfect choices to write high-quality letters of recommendation.

Many schools begin or end parent nights with group information sessions on a variety of topics, which can provide a deeper understanding of what is happening at the school, what resources are available to students, or what programs are specific to the school. Many of these information sessions are run by the guidance or college counseling departments, which presents another great opportunity for parents and students to build relationships that can pay off handsomely during the college application process.

College fairs, whether organized by your local high school, a regional confederation of schools or districts, or larger nonprofit education organizations such as the National Association for College Admission Counseling (NACAC), are events in which colleges and universities send representatives to a shared location, likely a local high school gym or a local convention center, in order to meet interested students. These representatives can be alumni volunteers but are often actual admissions officers. Attending a college fair allows students, and parents, to make an in-person connection with the schools that interest them but are far more likely to be local and convenient.

Parents can also participate in the college application process in other, sometimes surprising, ways. When a student takes a test preparation program for the SAT or ACT, there are often homework assignments and practice tests. Take a few moments to learn how to proctor a practice SAT or ACT, which can help students better prepare for the real deal.

Things to Avoid

As mentioned before, there are some obvious errors parents should avoid in the effort to guide their child through the college application process, such as bribing officials, cheating on standardized tests, or committing other related felonies, but even honest parents make mistakes. One of the most common mistakes I have observed parents make is interfering in the college application essay.

The college application essay is an important part of the college application process. How important depends on the student, the college, and the situation. Regardless of the differences in those factors, the essay provides college admissions officers valuable insight into the personal narrative applicants seek to create. Even when students are able to arrange for an in-person interview with an admissions officer, the essay provides an easily shared document to which admissions officers can refer throughout the application review process.

Since the essay is an important document, it is understandable that parents are concerned about the quality of the writing. Providing your child with constructive feedback can be invaluable in the drafting, revising, and editing of the essay. This is especially true since most adults have years and years of experience writing for work, even if only emails and other technical documents.

The trap lies in how much help parents provide to their children. The essay must be student written. As a parent, do not write the essay, or any part of it. Don't even rewrite sentences during an edit of the essay. The limit of what is acceptable is making suggestions, which can be ignored.

As a tutor, I have guided hundreds of students through the essay writing task. My job is to support the student through the steps in writing a successful college application essay, from selecting which question they will address, to brainstorming and outlining, all the way through drafting, revising, and editing the essay. Never once have I written even a piece of an essay for a student. Tutoring means teaching the student to do it on her own, and while I have suggested turns of phrase to students, it is always their choice. And sometimes the students chose to write what I considered mistakes.

During my time tutoring students on the college application essay, I have encountered essays written, or cowritten, by a parent, and my response is always the same. Erase and start over. The essay must be in the student's voice, and most importantly, it must be authentic and truthful. By "the student's voice" I mean that it must sound like the student wrote the essay, primarily by utilizing language, including vocabulary and grammar, that the student would actually use in a spontaneous conversation.

Authentic means representative of the lived experience of the student. The essay should tell a story that is not only based in truth, but is accurate to the culture, community, and background of the student. Whether a student comes from a background of privilege or poverty, there is no benefit in trying to hide that story. Colleges will know what high school the student attended, where she grew up, and what achievements she has accomplished, and they will know this because she told them in the application.

One more word on the concept of truthfulness and the phrase *based in truth*. The college application essay has a maximum length of 650 words. In the average paperback, whether you choose to read *The Great Gatsby* or the latest Dan Brown thriller, a page of a paperback contains an average of 400 words. That means that 650 words is approximately one and a half pages when typed. That is not a lot of space in which to introduce oneself to a college admissions officer and tell a compelling story that will encourage a college admissions officer to advocate on behalf of a student to other admissions officers.

Famed film director Alfred Hitchcock once said, "Drama is life with the dull bits cut out." Freddie Mercury, lead singer of the rock band Queen, lived for forty-five years. The movie about his life, *Bohemian Rhapsody*, has a running length of two hours and fourteen minutes. With this in mind, students must utilize various storytelling techniques in order to build the most compelling narrative in their essays. They will condense time, conflate events, and carefully select the bits that best tell the story. So long as all of the bits are true, the story is truthful.

Beyond the essay, the other big trap to avoid is setting unrealistic expectations. Not every student is going to attend Harvard, Yale, or Princeton. The good news is that not every student needs to attend Harvard, Yale, or Princeton in order to lead a joyful life. Again, there are over 4,300 colleges and universities in the United States, and they come in all types and sizes. Graduating college is the culmination of years of hard work and dedication, and to do so from any institution is an impressive accomplishment.

There is virtually no such thing as a bad college. So long as a student finds a school that has the program that she wants to study, the environment in which she wants to live for the next four years, and the culture that will nurture her along the way, then that is the best possible college for that student.

More importantly, there are no longer any guarantees about admission to the most prestigious colleges like those in the Ivy League. One hundred years ago, so long as a young man came from a background of wealth and privilege, he could find a spot at a prestigious college. Forty years ago, a combination of "perfect" SAT score and a high GPA was the gateway to Ivy League admission. Now, Harvard turns down more high school valedictorians than it accepts due to the enormous number of qualified applicants each year.

Rather than look at this fact with despair, I recommend seeing this as an opportunity to explore admissions at excellent colleges that are less well known to you, possibly more affordable, and definitely seeking highly motivated and academically qualified candidates. There are more colleges striving to attain the quality and reputation of an Ivy League school than there are Ivy League schools, and those up-and-coming colleges are working hard to attract the best faculty and students in order to build their reputations. Furthermore, they are often willing to spend the scholarship dollars to do it.

THE EIGHTEEN MONTH TESTING TIMELINE

In the following pages, you will find two versions of a testing timeline. The first is the timeline that students and parents normally follow, especially if they have never been given good advice from their school guidance counselor or a private college counselor. The second timeline is our recommended testing timeline. It is my opinion that the best plan is to start early and spread out the process in order to reduce stress and anxiety.

TRADITIONAL TIMELINE

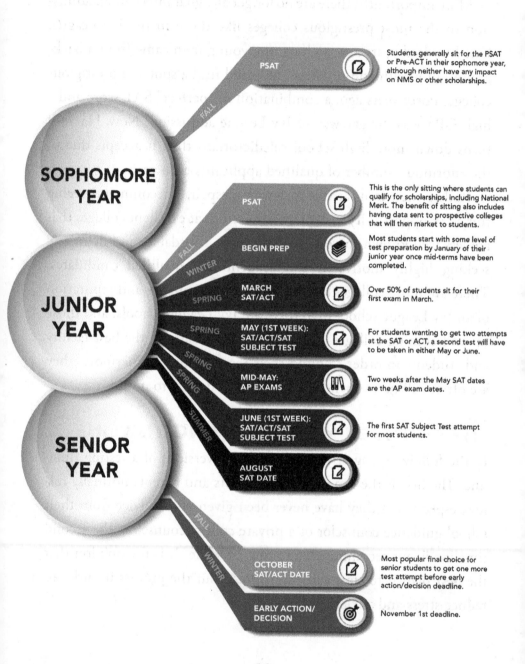

SOPHOMORE YEAR

PSAT — FALL
Students generally sit for the PSAT or Pre-ACT in their sophomore year, although neither have any impact on NMS or other scholarships.

JUNIOR YEAR

PSAT — FALL
This is the only sitting where students can qualify for scholarships, including National Merit. The benefit of sitting also includes having data sent to prospective colleges that will then market to students.

BEGIN PREP — WINTER
Most students start with some level of test preparation by January of their junior year once mid-terms have been completed.

MARCH SAT/ACT — SPRING
Over 50% of students sit for their first exam in March.

MAY (1ST WEEK): SAT/ACT/SAT SUBJECT TEST — SPRING
For students wanting to get two attempts at the SAT or ACT, a second test will have to be taken in either May or June.

MID-MAY: AP EXAMS — SPRING
Two weeks after the May SAT dates are the AP exam dates.

JUNE (1ST WEEK): SAT/ACT/SAT SUBJECT TEST — SUMMER
The first SAT Subject Test attempt for most students.

AUGUST SAT DATE

SENIOR YEAR

OCTOBER SAT/ACT DATE — FALL
Most popular final choice for senior students to get one more test attempt before early action/decision deadline.

EARLY ACTION/ DECISION — WINTER
November 1st deadline.

IDEAL TIMELINE

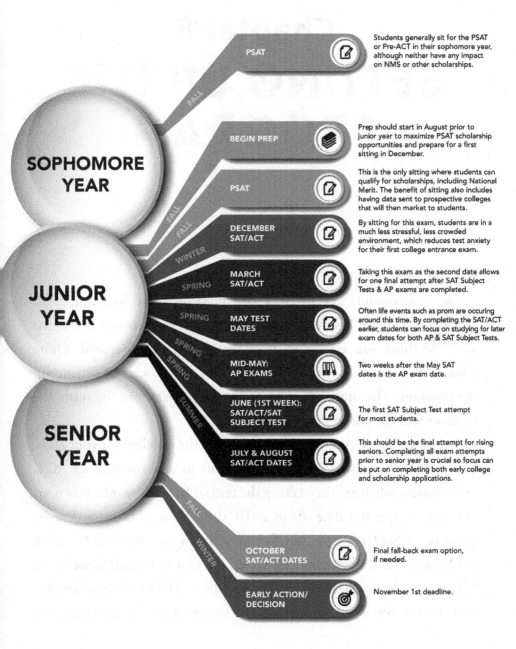

SOPHOMORE YEAR

JUNIOR YEAR

SENIOR YEAR

PSAT — Students generally sit for the PSAT or Pre-ACT in their sophomore year, although neither have any impact on NMS or other scholarships.

BEGIN PREP — Prep should start in August prior to junior year to maximize PSAT scholarship opportunities and prepare for a first sitting in December.

PSAT — This is the only sitting where students can qualify for scholarships, including National Merit. The benefit of sitting also includes having data sent to prospective colleges that will then market to students.

DECEMBER SAT/ACT — By sitting for this exam, students are in a much less stressful, less crowded environment, which reduces test anxiety for their first college entrance exam.

MARCH SAT/ACT — Taking this exam as the second date allows for one final attempt after SAT Subject Tests & AP exams are completed.

MAY TEST DATES — Often life events such as prom are occuring around this time. By completing the SAT/ACT earlier, students can focus on studying for later exam dates for both AP & SAT Subject Tests.

MID-MAY: AP EXAMS — Two weeks after the May SAT dates is the AP exam date.

JUNE (1ST WEEK): SAT/ACT/SAT SUBJECT TEST — The first SAT Subject Test attempt for most students.

JULY & AUGUST SAT/ACT DATES — This should be the final attempt for rising seniors. Completing all exam attempts prior to senior year is crucial so focus can be put on completing both early college and scholarship applications.

OCTOBER SAT/ACT DATES — Final fall-back exam option, if needed.

EARLY ACTION/ DECISION — November 1st deadline.

Chapter 8
SETTING UP THE PROGRAM

INTRODUCTION

A successful SAT or ACT test prep program does not begin when the first lesson starts. If the first class session is the first thing you are doing, then you're not truly prepared. Quite a bit of thought and effort should go into the process of setting up the program. The more effort you put into preparation, the more the students will get out of the class.

Before anything else, you must decide on the timeline for your class. The goal of the class is to prepare students to take the SAT or ACT. Ask yourself, when are they taking the test(s)? In other words, you need to select a target test date. As of 2019, the SAT is administered seven times per school year: the last Saturday in August; the first Saturday in October, November, and December; the first or second Saturday in March; and the first Saturday in May and June. The ACT is also administered seven times per school year: the second Saturday in September;

the last Saturday in October; and the second Saturday in December, February, April, June, and July.

Please be aware that these dates are subject to change. In fact, the College Board only added the August test date in 2017, replacing a relatively unpopular January test date. ACT Inc. added the July test date in 2018, bringing the number of administrations of the ACT to seven per year for the first time. Additionally, the March SAT test date has been administered in April on rare occasions when Easter and Passover fell very early in the calendar. In 2020, the College Board added a one-time September test date on the last Saturday of the month to make up for the cancelled test dates the previous spring due to the coronavirus pandemic crisis.

Your timeline not only includes the considered the target test date but includes time enough for students to complete homework in between sessions. Practice and review are essential to developing mastery of the skills taught in the program. Assigning homework allows the students to practice without wasting valuable class time with long stretches with no actual instruction.

Additionally, you will likely want to block out some time for practice tests. Not only does a practice test either late in the program or after the program has ended provide useful data on how the students are doing after instruction, but a practice test before instruction can provide a baseline score from which you and your students can game-plan a goal and gauge progress throughout the program.

SCHEDULE

Once you decide which SAT or ACT test date is the targeted test date, you can begin to build your schedule. Work backwards from the targeted test date to determine when you need to begin your program.

This sounds like an easy task, but environmental factors unique to your situation can quickly complicate building a schedule.

I have taught SAT and ACT classes in all sorts of schools, tutoring centers, and temporary locations utilized by nonprofit organizations, and no two programs have ever been the same. This is mostly due to the schedules dictated by the varying needs of and obstacles faced by each organization running the classes. Each type of institution has different facilities available to them which can impose different types of availability restrictions. Restrictions, however, can lead to inspiration and innovation in scheduling your program.

The most common solution is to schedule a weekly class. The average amount of time for an SAT or ACT program runs between twenty and thirty hours of instruction. Select a day of the week, a time of day, and a class session length. The class session length, along with how often in a week the class meets, will determine how many weeks in advance of the target test date the class should begin.

Imagine an SAT class that targets the March test date, at a school which will be hosting the class on Saturday mornings for an opt-in population of students. Regardless of whether ten or a hundred students enroll in such a class, the schedule will look relatively the same. I do recommend, however, that should you host a test prep class in which dozens or hundreds of students are enrolled, please split up the students into different sections. Test prep is not a subject that works well in a large lecture hall format.

Balancing budgetary and academic considerations, you have decided on a twenty-four-hour program. At this point, you have the option to arrange the program into either twelve two-hour class sessions or eight three-hour class sessions. I would recommend the twelve two-hour class session option in order to slow down the program, reduce student stress, and increase the number of learning opportunities. However, no one will judge you for doing what is right for your students, school, or community.

Now that we have selected twelve two-hour sessions for our imaginary class, we can begin to schedule the sessions. Use your calendar to count back thirteen Saturdays before the next March test date, which is usually the second Saturday of the month. In those thirteen Saturdays, you will schedule the twelve class sessions and a practice test. Some classes hold the practice test in the final week before the actual SAT, while others hold the practice test one to three weeks before that. The difference is that holding a practice test with class sessions remaining allows the instructor(s) and students to review the results of the practice test in class.

Now that you know the dates of the class sessions, pick out a time of day. For weekend classes, mornings are usually best, since students should be fresh from a full night's sleep and a healthy breakfast. Some of the schools with which I have worked have opted instead to host weekly classes as an after-school program. While these programs have been successful, I strongly recommend inserting some break time between the end of the school day and the start of the test prep class session. Student performance increases after a break, especially when students have the time for a snack and to get out some of their energy following a long day of learning.

When counting back the thirteen Saturdays before the target test date, don't forget to account for holidays and school vacations. While many school districts and states schedule spring break in March, some schools, districts, and states schedule vacation weeks during other times. Public schools in Massachusetts, for example, often take a full week of vacation during mid-February, beginning with Presidents' Day.

To finish our example, let's look at this sample calendar below for the months leading up to March 2020. Let's imagine that the school that is scheduling this program is in Massachusetts, so we will need to account for the February break, as well as winter break. The SAT we chose was scheduled to be administered on March 14, 2020.

Class Session 1: Saturday, November 16, 2019
Class Session 2: Saturday, November 23, 2019
Class Session 3: Saturday, December 7, 2019
Class Session 4: Saturday, December 14, 2019
Class Session 5: Saturday, December 21, 2019
Class Session 6: Saturday, January 4, 2020
Class Session 7: Saturday, January 11, 2020
Class Session 8: Saturday, January 18, 2020
Class Session 9: Saturday, January 25, 2020
Practice Test: Saturday, February 1, 2020
Class Session 10: Saturday, February 8, 2020
Class Session 11: Saturday, February 29, 2020
Class Session 12: Saturday, March 7, 2020

Notice how this schedule accounts for not only the two Saturdays during the week of February break, but the Saturdays during winter break and the Saturday during Thanksgiving weekend. I have noticed that accounting for these holiday weekends in the schedule is the factor that surprises students and parents the most about a test prep class schedule. Many families don't realize the classes need to begin this far in advance of a target test date in order to not only account for all of the class sessions and a practice test, but real life as well.

The benefits of hosting a class on the weekend include flexibility in scheduling the class, including hosting multiple sections throughout the day. Not only are morning classes an option on a Saturday or Sunday, but you can stack classes throughout the day to accommodate a large number of students, especially if you find yourself scrambling to find qualified instructors. Take a look back at the sample calendar schedule. You can host a 10:00 a.m.–12:00 p.m. class each day, and then if you have more than a dozen students enrolled, you can either host two concurrent sections beginning at 10:00 a.m., or if you only have one instructor available, host the second section beginning at 1:00 p.m., providing a nice lunch break to your instructor.

The biggest drawback to weekend classes that I have encountered is participation. Weekend classes are by definition opt in. Whether you are a teacher, counselor, or administrator at a school, or you are a staff member at a nonprofit organization, you cannot require students to attend a class on a weekend. Even when parents and students sign up for a weekend test prep class, even one that is offered for free by your school, should you choose to assume the entire cost of the program, attendance is likely to be spotty, even accounting for holiday weekends. This is why some schools and nonprofit organizations choose to host classes after school on a weekday.

Weekday classes have the definite benefit of increasing attendance for students who have enrolled. The students are already on campus or at your facility, so it is much easier to convince students to stick around for class. In my observation, after-school classes tend to have more consistent attendance than weekend classes.

The downsides to an after-school program should be fairly self-evident. Students in an after-school test prep class are more likely to be burned out from a long day of school. After-school programs are also more likely to conflict with other, usually more fun, activities like sports practice or performance rehearsal. Additionally, it is more difficult to stack class sessions back-to-back on the same day to account for different sections should more than a dozen students enroll in the program.

You can choose to host different sections concurrently, if you have more than one instructor, or host different sections on different days of the week if there is only one instructor available. What is unlikely to work, however, is attempting to host a 3:00 p.m.–5:00 p.m. class and then a 6:00 p.m.–8:00 p.m. class. By that point, students will have gone home, hopefully to get a good meal and complete their homework. It is difficult to get students to come back to school for a 6:00 p.m. class once they have gone home when school lets out at 2:30 p.m.

One solution that some schools have settled on is an in-school weekday program. Hosting a program during the school day can solve many of the problems posed by after-school or weekend programs. The students are much more of a captive audience, and participation is much higher for opt-in programs. Many schools, especially when the program is a budgeted course, and therefore entirely free for the students and their families, add the program to the schedule as an opt-out course as part of the guidance/college counseling program. Schools which choose to do this effectively end up offering the test prep program to their entire junior class.

This level of participation poses both great opportunities and challenging conundrums. Sharing a solid test prep program with your entire junior class, rather than a small group of students who have opted in, helps you build up valuable data about the performance of your junior class on standardized tests. After several years, you will have a treasure trove of data which can guide you in your decision-making processes. Furthermore, the score improvements that the students see will help them reach for their goals with more confidence, which could have ripple effects on performance in other areas. I have seen this in classes I have taught. I have worked with students who did not believe they had any hope of earning admission to college, but seeing an improvement from their PSAT result to a postclass SAT result they didn't expect inspired them to dedicate themselves more to their studies. Clearly, these students did all of the work that helped them improve their grades, apply to colleges they previously thought beyond their reach, and achieve acceptances, but the course I taught helped build the confidence they needed to start their journey, and that is what inspires me to share my experience in test prep here.

The conundrum is how to serve an entire junior class in a weekly test prep program. Clearly, you can't merely fill the school auditorium and hope that any student will get anything out of a class like that. A solution I have experienced at a school where I have taught test prep was to arrange the test prep program through a required "elective" class called College Counseling. The juniors were sorted into five relatively equal-sized sections of approximately twenty students, each of which had the College Counseling class once per week, each week from the beginning of the school year through the March SAT test date. Since the class periods were forty-five minutes in length, the students attended a total of twenty-five class sessions, for a total in-class engagement of 18.75 hours of instruction.

While a little short compared to the ideal instructional time, the students at this particular school saw an average improvement of approximately 100 points from their PSAT results to their final SAT results. Given that a typical junior class is going to have a large variation in effort and skill, I am quite proud of the results I achieved with that school. Additionally, the high-performing students saw larger increases, improving the school's count of students exceeding both the 1,500 and 1,400 score thresholds over previous graduating classes.

Of course, not every school has the ability to schedule a once-per-week class across multiple quarters, marking periods, trimesters, or semesters. Alternately, you can schedule a test prep class during a particular block or period five days per week (or within a rotating block schedule) within a single quarter.

A class that begins after the PSAT, at the beginning of the second quarter, may start during the first week of November, continue through December into mid-January, ending at midterms. This course could have thirty-five to forty sessions (depending on holiday breaks and other days off) of forty-five minutes each for a total student engagement of approximately twenty-six to thirty instructional hours.

The biggest logistical difference between the two options is that a once-a-week class with five sections per week can be taught by a single instructor. Holding five sections daily would either require five instructors to teach the course concurrently, or a full-time teacher to teach the course five different times throughout the day.

Another concern about fitting a test prep course into a single quarter is that the school year quarters rarely line up with an SAT test date. The example I described of the second quarter course would end in mid-January, approximately six to seven weeks before the March test date. That would leave plenty of time for students to review and practice on their own, but the sad truth is that the majority of students won't review or practice. That's the whole reason that test prep is so powerful. If students were self-motivated enough to practice on their own, they would all be using Khan Academy for SAT prep, and we know that most students are not.

An additional option is the week-long intensive class, sometimes called a boot camp. This is a very popular option for programs hosted over the summer or during vacation weeks throughout the school year. A common boot camp schedule I have used over the years is Monday through Friday with class sessions from 9:00 a.m. to 12:00 p.m. and 1:00 p.m. to 4:00 p.m. each day. The typical boot camp I have taught is a thirty-hour course, especially when the target test date is some weeks after the class has ended.

Summer boot camps often target the August SAT test date or the September ACT test date. School vacation boot camps will target the next administration of the SAT or ACT. Either way, since all of the instruction takes place within the confines of one calendar week, decisions about administering a practice test or review sessions must be addressed. The center owner of one of the tutoring centers at which I worked often sold the boot camp program bundled with a Saturday practice test so that families were prepared for a six-day class experience. Another tutoring facility at which I worked hosted a large end-of-summer practice test at a local high school so that all of the summer boot camp students would get a practice test as close to the autumn test dates as possible. Find the solution that works best for your situation.

Boot camps can be great experiences for students, especially when you or your instructor(s) work to build a collaborative and fun environment. A boot camp is almost like SAT summer camp, if designed and managed with the right attitude. Whenever I have taught a summer SAT or ACT boot camp, I have supplemented content instruction with college counseling information, including fun videos and discussions. Additionally, the camaraderie that a boot camp fosters can lead to students building relationships that can be beneficial when discussing and critiquing the essays.

Boot camps do have their downsides as well. Not every student makes the most progress on their standardized test results through a class, which is why one-on-one instruction is so popular. A boot camp only exacerbates the situation as students receive a huge amount of information in a short amount of time. This is especially true for a boot camp that ends several weeks before a targeted test date. A July boot camp targeting the September ACT, October PSAT, or October SAT, can still impart valuable information, but that value is offset by the long break between the end of instruction and the test date.

The August SAT date has solved some of these concerns. At one tutoring center where I worked, the center owner scheduled a free three-hour booster class for the SAT program the weekend before the October test date each year. This was, of course, before the College Board introduced the August test date in 2017. Booster classes can be a satisfying solution regardless of the test date. Many school districts, for example, have their spring break in mid-March, after the March SAT test date. A boot camp held during that week would target either the April ACT or May SAT dates by necessity. Holding a three-hour booster class in early April for the ACT or in late April for the SAT could bolster the results that students see and build confidence in your program amongst the various stakeholders: students, parents, teachers, administrators, and so forth.

The choice between a weekly class or a boot camp is a serious existential question for a test prep class. The course, materials, and instruction are usually the same, so other considerations, such as space, time, personnel, and resources often play a larger role in this decision. Regardless of which format and schedule you choose, preplanning is the key to a successful experience for all involved.

SPACE

Just because you have created a schedule for a test program, including making decisions on the format, does not mean you are ready to start. There are several other considerations to keep in mind as you set up your test prep program. Once you know when you want to hold your program, you must acquire a space in which to hold your program.

On the one hand, all you really need is a room with some tables and chairs—places for the students to sit and something on which they can rest the books and write in them. If that is all you have available to you, then that is good enough to start.

Space considerations mean more than just having a room. The size of the room will determine how many students you can accommodate in a class section. Test prep, like academic courses, is not meant for a standing-room-only audience. Test prep classes are not supposed to be lectures. They should be conversations. All of the classes I have taught were managed in more of a seminar format. Student participation is essential to a successful class. A space that doesn't allow for interaction between instructor and student is not a space conducive to a successful program.

While technology, which I will discuss in more detail later in this chapter, can be helpful in a test prep class, it is not essential. Don't let access to technology preclude an otherwise comfortable space from providing a home for your test prep class.

Especially when you choose to go low tech, one resource that is incredibly important to communicating information is a whiteboard, or dry-erase board, at the front of the classroom. If the space available to you does not come with a whiteboard or other large, flat surface on which to write information, you should invest in a portable white-board at a size large enough to be seen from the back of the room.

While verbal instruction is a part of the program, visuals are a powerful tool in instruction, and are a core part of the delivery of a successful test prep program.

Because space can be at a premium in certain environments and in certain communities, I strongly recommend reserving or booking your space six months to a year in advance of the course. Even if the program in question is at a school, and all of the facilities are controlled and managed by a single administrative team, conflicts or other claims to a viable teaching space can arise.

Once you select a space and reserve it, you can begin to consider other aspects of setting up a test prep program.

PREPROGRAM SCORES

The goal of a test prep program is to help students improve their SAT or ACT results as a tool for improving their college application packages. This goal does not presume a particular result in a vacuum, but an improvement over a preprogram score. Framing the goal as an improvement from a score achieved before the program begins is due to how colleges consider SAT and ACT scores. Generally, colleges do not have a cutoff result that precludes students who have scored below that score from gaining admission. Instead, colleges consider a range of scores as acceptable, depending on other factors in a student's application package, such as grades or GPA, the level of difficulty of the student's high school classes, extracurricular activities, and personal narrative.

Since there is no one score to achieve, but instead a range of scores, no two students will have the same goal. The goal is built from two factors: the twenty-fifth to seventy-fifth percentile range of a favored college and a previous test score. The previous test score is the starting place for each individual student. This previous score can be a practice test score, preferably achieved by taking an actual-conditions practice test. The most accurate, and useful, previous score will come from an official testing, such as a real SAT or ACT result or, more likely, a PSAT or PreACT result.

A PSAT or PreACT result is often the best preprogram score from which to build a student's goal. The PSAT and PreACT are official tests, administered through the student's school, and scored by the College Board or ACT Inc., respectively. The data published in the score report is as accurate and official as possible.

The results of taking a real SAT or ACT prior to beginning a program would serve just as well as those of the PSAT or PreACT. However, since the majority of high school students don't take their first SAT or ACT until spring of their junior year, those results are often too late to serve as preprogram scores.

In the rare occasions when an official result, such as the PSAT or PreACT, is not available, students can use a full-length practice test as a preprogram score. There are several flaws with using practice tests. First, it is often a waste of a good practice test to use one of the official practice tests published by the College Board or ACT Inc. in their official practice test books. I recommend saving all of the available official practice tests for homework or in-class assignments. Official materials are going to be superior to any third-party practice material since they are official.

This is why I also don't recommend using third-party practice tests for the preprogram score. Third-party tests are never as accurate as they would need to be to provide a diagnostic or predictive result from which to create a goal score or a program of private, one-to-one instruction. I have never found an SAT or ACT practice test by a third-party publisher that matched the real tests accurately.

There is one exception to this: the comparison test. Many organizations, including Livius, the company for which I currently work, have created comparison tests. In these exams, a sampling of SAT-like and ACT-like questions are used to help students and families determine which of the two major college admission exams is a better fit for the student. Generally, these types of practice exams are not particularly good at predicting performance, but they usually do a good job helping students compare the experience on the two tests.

Luckily, more and more schools are administering an official PSAT or PreACT during the autumn of sophomore year. Schools have been encouraged by both the College Board and ACT Inc. to do so for various reasons that have nothing to do with test prep. For example, the College Board claims that the PSAT, when administered during October of sophomore year, is the best predictor of success in AP classes. I don't necessarily follow their logic, as I have found that consistent high performance in honors-level classes over two to three years can be a good predictor of success in an AP level class in any given topic. That being said, many school districts and high schools have jumped on the bandwagon of the sophomore-year PSAT or PreACT testing, especially since the data produced by these tests help schools plan out their guidance and college counseling programs.

Since many, if not most, of the students in your program, whether the program is hosted by a school or district, a nonprofit organization, or a homeschooling collective, will have taken a real PSAT or PreACT during sophomore year, you can begin a test prep program as early as the summer before junior year. This should help alleviate some of the stress of choosing a format, building a schedule, and selecting a location for your program.

With an accurate preprogram score, you can help students select a reasonable and achievable goal either during the program, which I recommend, or prior to the program during the enrollment process. I like to fold the goal-setting process into my instruction during the introductory lesson when I teach an SAT or ACT class. This often leads to a discussion among the students about colleges that interest them, which can introduce a student to a school she has never heard of before.

MATERIALS

I have taught SAT and ACT classes in all types of environments for a variety of different types of organizations. Whether I worked with a large corporation or a small nonprofit, the single most important resource in these classes was the course materials. Course materials include both instructional materials and practice problems. I can teach a successful test prep course without access to technology, in too small a space, or without adequate institutional support. The lack of instructional material and practice problems will doom a program.

Practice material is far easier to acquire than instructional material. Both the College Board and ACT Inc. publish prep guides with full-length official practice tests. The College Board's *Official SAT Study Guide* currently contains eight full-length practice tests, each of which is followed by detailed explanations of the correct answer for each question. The explanations are often pedantic and technical; I find that it is simpler to solve the questions strategically; however, some explanation is better than none. Oddly, the College Board's book does not include simple answer keys.

The College Board has released eight practice tests as PDF documents on their website, all of which are identical to tests in the College

Board's book. I have often found it more cost effective, when working at a school or with a nonprofit, to have the students download the practice test PDFs rather than purchase their own copy of the College Board's book. The book costs between twenty-five and thirty dollars, depending on where you purchase it, which may be prohibitive for certain students. This can be also be an overwhelming expense for a school or nonprofit which is providing a class for no cost to families. In addition to each individual practice test, both a simple answer key and a packet of explanations are available to download from the College Board's website.

Despite all of this, the book is often the best solution for students. Not only will students find all eight practice tests in one place, the College Board book includes some instructional material before the practice tests. Most of the College Board's instructional material is fairly weak, in my opinion; however, the section on the essay is very useful, both for the two sample essay prompts and a collection of example responses that can be quite illuminating.

Either way you or your students acquire copies of the official practice tests, they represent the absolute best homework and practice material available for the SAT. No matter how good practice tests published by third parties may seem, only the real thing is really good enough. As you will see in the sample syllabus later in this chapter and the instructional materials in chapter 10, I generally recommend saving the official SAT practice tests for homework assignments or a full-length practice test. Try not to waste the official tests as in-class instructional material.

At different times, the College Board has released two free practice PSAT tests as well. Both were available on the College Board website at different times. If you can find either of them on the internet, I recommend utilizing them as in-class instructional or practice material. Practice PSATs don't make for good full-length practice sections or tests for an SAT program, since PSATs are both shorter and represent content that is slightly easier than what students will see on a real SAT. Official PSAT practice tests do make good instructional and sample problems, though, since the PSAT and the SAT are relatively similar.

ACT Inc. also publishes a book of practice tests, *The Official ACT Prep Guide*, but their book only contains five full-length tests. Additionally, ACT Inc. only posts a single practice test on their website. Whether for good or ill, it is a completely different test than any of the five in their book. Interestingly, ACT Inc. updates the free, downloadable practice test every two to three years, removing the old free test in favor of a new one. Since the 2016 updates to the ACT, the organization has released two free downloadable practice tests. If you are not aware, ACT Inc. has a unique naming system for their practice tests based on the year the test was published or administered and a code representing the particular version of the test. The free practice ACT released in 2015, shortly before the new version of the ACT was first administered to students on an actual test date, was called 1572C, while the most recently released free practice test is called 1874F. Both of these practice tests are useful supplements to the five tests available in the prep guide.

You may have noticed that there are noticeably fewer practice tests available for the ACT than for the SAT. This is exacerbated by the fact that ACT Inc. has never released a practice PreACT either on paper or on the internet. So, while you may be able to utilize up to two full-length practice PSATs to supplement the eight officially released practice SATs, you cannot do the same for the ACT. Luckily, the instructional material in *The Official ACT Prep Guide* is very good, generally much better than the instructional material in the College Board's SAT book. You can also find additional sample problems on the ACT website. The same is true for the SAT on College Board's website.

Depending on the length of the program you put together for your students, you will likely not need more practice tests than what either College Board or ACT Inc. have published. In my experience, I have found that the sections in four to five practice tests are sufficient for in-class practice and homework assignments. In fact, a major mistake that many instructors make is just assigning one section after another or one full-length practice test after another, without taking the time to review individual questions or review and reinforce strategies. Administering practice tests to a class but not reviewing the results all the way down to discussing individual questions has no educational value. In my opinion, an instructor should spend as much time reviewing homework assignments as possible.

When additional instructional materials are necessary, I recommend using content-based materials. Rather than just assigning more SAT or ACT practice sets, dive into the content covered on the test, whether reading comprehension, grammar, or math skills. The important thing to remember is that a test prep program should be a strategies-first program, in which test-taking skills and other study skills are taught first. Use content-based instruction as a supplement to test-taking instruction since neither the SAT nor the ACT introduce new content to students, and instead depend on students remembering content they have learned over the previous four to five years. All content instruction for an SAT or ACT program is content review.

If you do find yourself needing additional full-length practice tests for your test prep program, you will be tempted to pick up copies of a third-party book. I understand if you feel you have no choice, but just remember my previous warning that third-party practice tests are never going to be as accurate compared to the real thing as the officially released practice tests. Instead, what some people have done is collect or acquire copies of actually administered tests that the College Board or ACT Inc. have released afterwards.

Several times per year, the College Board offers what they call the question and answer service (QAS). When registering for the SAT, a student or parent can pay an extra fee during a QAS administration, and upon receiving the score report in the mail students will also receive a copy of the actual test they took several weeks earlier. Historically, the College Board has offered the QAS during the October, March, and May test dates. ACT Inc. offers a similar fee-based service.

Various independent tutors, high school guidance counseling offices, and third-party websites have collected these QAS tests, which can be found on the internet from time to time. Both College Board and ACT Inc. spend a great deal of time and energy removing old QAS tests from the internet. Sharing a QAS test you have acquired with your students is a gray area, which may violate copyright law. Selling access to such tests is a definite violation of copyright law, so I strongly advise students, parents, tutors, and school administrators not to ever sell a QAS SAT or ACT test under any circumstances, or to charge students or families for a practice test administration.

TECHNOLOGY

In my career, I have taught test prep classes for the SAT and ACT in public schools, with for-profit corporations, and at poorly funded non-profit organizations. In some places, I have had access to amazing technology that simplified labor-intensive processes, allowing me to focus exclusively on teaching. In other places, I have spent more time than I would like scoring practice tests and homework sections by hand due to the lack of technology. Technology doesn't teach students, but it can make certain aspects of teaching less arduous and time consuming.

I have never been prevented from teaching a test prep class by the lack of technology. I have found, however, that certain technological tools can make teaching simpler and more effective. The single most effective time-saving technological tool that I recommend is an overhead projector. Since most of the practice and example materials you will be using are available as PDFs, you can often project practice or homework problems onto a whiteboard. Rather than wasting time transcribing wordy math problems or chunks of reading and grammar passages onto the board, a simple projection can save time by getting directly to the instruction. At schools which have them, digital smart-boards serve the same purpose.

The point of assigning full-length practice sections as homework is not only to build the students' facility with the strategies and content of the tests, but also to gauge progress. Tracking how a student is doing on homework or practice sections can inform your instruction and guide you in making adjustments during a program. Scoring full sections by hand is time consuming and arduous. Several third-party companies offer internet services for scoring the officially released SAT and ACT practice test sections. If that is not an option, setting up a simple Excel spreadsheet can make scoring a homework section or practice test less painful and more productive. It is a hassle to set up a spreadsheet to score sections, and often involves a learning curve on the part of the students, but it can provide a quick snapshot of how a student is doing.

Calculators are allowed on both the SAT and the ACT, and many students already have sophisticated calculators which they use in their high-level math classes in school. Just as many students don't have access to advanced graphing calculators due to a lack of funds or access to advanced math courses. Luckily, the most sophisticated calculators are not necessary on the SAT or ACT. A basic scientific calculator, usually available in stores for less than twenty dollars per unit, is more than enough for either test. In fact, simple calculators available at the dollar store can be used with great success on both tests.

Since both the SAT and ACT are currently paper-based tests, access to a reliable photocopier is useful. Often, it is cheaper and more efficient to make copies of sample problems rather than purchasing entire books of practice tests for students. Use your best judgment and remember that paying for books supports those who write the books, making updated editions more likely.

Access to a computer for instructional slide decks or to share content from the College Board or ACT website can provide extra educational value to students during a class session. Of course, this is not a necessity for a successful class. Any qualified instructor should be able to communicate the appropriate strategies and content regardless of access to technology.

Of course, technology might prove to be essential to teaching a successful test prep program, as we all recently learned during the 2020 coronavirus pandemic crisis. Due to social distancing and stay-in-place orders issued by governors and mayors across the United States, schools, tutoring centers, and other educational facilities were forced to pivot to online instruction. In order to deliver academic content to students at home, schools and other educational organizations invested in remote learning and video chat platforms offered by Google, Microsoft, Apple, Zoom, Twiddla, and others.

Regardless of the outcome of the 2020 coronavirus pandemic crisis, the educational landscape has been altered forever. As an educator, administrator, parent, or student, you might find the best solution for building and executing a test prep program is to hold it remotely over the internet. In this case, you are stuck with depending on technology. Make sure to find a platform that works for you for meeting with and sharing information with your students.

OTHER RESOURCES

To build a successful test prep program, an instructor needs access to a few basic items, as I've already mentioned. An instructor needs a plan, which means a syllabus and lesson plans, some of which are described later in this chapter. An instructor needs practice materials and homework sets, the best of which are found in the official practice test books published by the College Board and ACT Inc. An instructor needs a classroom space in which students can safely and productively work and learn. Anything beyond that can enhance a program but should not be considered the minimum viable program.

That being said, additional resources can solve certain problems for instructors and students. Beyond the technologies listed in the previous section of this chapter, there are other tools and technologies which can save time and provide educational benefits to the students.

As noted in the previous section, some companies have built section scoring interfaces on the internet, accessible in a regular web browser, for scoring sections of the SAT or ACT. Finding one of these services that is both free and easy to use can take some research on the part of an instructor or program administrator. Especially for schools and nonprofits with tight budgets, it is difficult to justify signing up for a fee-based service to score homework sections, but many of these services have intuitive interfaces and generate easy-to-read score reports. Rather than recommend one such service over another, I will merely state that I have utilized several of these services, and the time saved by students or instructors can be worth a small investment.

If you find yourself meeting with students over the internet, you will be tempted to use a free video chat service such as Skype. Such a service is often the best choice for an individual meeting with a single student at a time. The downside is that free services are often technologically unstable or hobbled by limitations. Some services impose time limits on free accounts, for example. For a homeschooling situation, it may be wise for an instructor to invest a small amount of money in a paid account with a robust service that has digital whiteboard tools built in.

For long-term programs, there is always the concern about running out of material. Most classroom-based programs are short enough that the practice tests published by the College Board or ACT Inc. usually last through the length of the course. Some instructors struggle, however, to find quality content-based material for their programs. Some schools, in fact, require instructors to include content-based instruction in the course. In this case, my best recommendation is to use the free resources at Khan Academy. Founded by educator Salman Khan in 2008, the service utilizes a series of videos and practice problems to help students build their content skills. College Board has partnered with Khan Academy to provide lessons and sample problems for SAT content. This material is a valuable resource for independent instructors and both schools and nonprofits operating under tight budget constraints. While ACT Inc. has not directly partnered with Khan Academy, there is quite a bit of material on the platform that overlaps with the content of the ACT. Additionally, both the College Board and ACT Inc. post sample problems on their own websites.

INSTRUCTORS

There are two indispensable factors in a successful test prep program: the instructional materials and the instructor. The right combination of the two can result in a program which not only prepares students for the SAT and/or the ACT but can elevate a program into an experience that inspires students long after the last standardized test is in students' metaphorical rearview mirror. I can still remember my own test prep experience during the summer before my junior year of high school. Even though the course was overloaded with more than forty students, the two instructors—one for math and one for verbal—instructed, implored, cajoled, entertained, and inspired us.

The majority of my adult life has been spent in the classroom, teaching and tutoring students, in both public school and private tutoring settings. I have learned so much from the act of teaching, both about how to connect with students and about myself. With more than twenty years of teaching experience under my belt, I am confident that I can teach any student in any environment.

Unfortunately, I am probably not available to teach your test prep class, especially if it is more than an hour drive from the Boston metropolitan area. Luckily, you don't need me to teach your class. Whether you are a student or parent looking for tips on how to teach a program at home, the instructor setting up a program at a school or nonprofit, or an administrator looking to hire or assign an instructor to your class, there are plenty of good teachers all around you.

The SAT and the ACT do not contain specialized material that only a select few can teach. These tests are called "standardized tests" for a reason. They actually depend on general reading, writing, and math knowledge for the content basis for the different sections. All middle school and high school teachers can handle the majority of the content on the two tests, especially with a little investment in brushing up on a few topics.

In fact, most adults with good communication skills can learn to teach a program for the SAT or the ACT. The biggest fear about teaching such programs that new instructors have shared with me is self-doubt regarding the math content on the tests. It is true that there are always a few very challenging math questions that include higher-level concepts from Algebra 2 or beginning precalculus on the test, but only a small percentage of students will be scoring high enough to worry about those problems, especially if your students hail from a historically underserved population.

The vast majority of students taking a test prep course need work in general test-taking skills, problem-solving skills, and study skills. That is the focus of a good test prep program. And that should be the focus of a test prep instructor. My background is in history, literature, and creative writing, and even though I am certified as a middle school math teacher, I do not feel qualified to teach most high school–level math courses. I can solve almost any SAT or ACT math problem, but I am not technically the best instructor for students who have extremely high starting math scores and who are looking to pick off those few high-level math problems. There are other instructors I know who are better qualified to help that tiny minority of students. Instead, I work best with the large pool of students whose starting scores are in the middle of the range.

In order to find the best instructor for your students, get to know them and their needs. When I have worked at high-end private tutoring centers, I know that I have to recruit, hire, and train high-level instructors who can handle the most challenging math problems. When I have worked at small nonprofits in the inner city, I have focused on finding tutors who can inspire students who have been told all their lives that they are not going to make anything of themselves. In those environments, an instructor's mastery of the material is very important, but still secondary to their ability to connect with the students.

Ultimately, a successful instructor is a good communicator. Regardless of how brilliant a person is, if they cannot effectively communicate what they know to one or more students, then all that knowledge is not useful in that moment. I have worked with some brilliant minds, both as a student and as a colleague, who could not teach, despite a deep well of knowledge coupled with prestigious advanced degrees. It takes a strongly dedicated student to overcome a teacher's terrible communication skills, and you can see this in action at colleges and universities around the world. College students and graduate students put in herculean effort to get the most out of working with brilliant professors who may not be good teachers.

High school students taking a test prep course are not in that situation. Most high school students enrolled in a test prep course are there because someone made them do it, whether it was their parents or school administrators. Test prep is not fun. It is not exciting. It is a chore, and most kids would rather be doing almost anything else than sitting in a test prep class or tutoring session.

An inspiring and fun instructor can make all the difference to a student whose mom and dad made them sign up for a test prep class. Find a good teacher and then provide that teacher with a clear and specific course to teach, and the class will be successful. More than math or writing skills, good improvisational skills are the key to a good test prep instructor. Technology fails. Books arrive late. Glitches happen. A calm and confident teacher will adapt and make the class successful regardless of any chaos going on around her or him.

SYLLABI AND LESSON PLANS

In order to provide the instructor with the best chance of success helping the students improve their test prep results, a clear and specific program of study is essential. A successful course of study begins with a syllabus. A syllabus is a guide to what the students are expected to learn over the course of the program. Building a syllabus begins with knowing how long the class will be, including how many sessions and the length of each session. In my experience working with tutoring centers, schools (whether public, private, or charter) and nonprofit organizations, I have noticed that organizations tend to build test prep programs on three models: the boot camp, the weekly class, and the school-day program.

In the Schedule section of this chapter, I described the most common format for a boot camp: the thirty-hour version. I have also taught boot camps in fifteen-, eighteen-, and twenty-four-hour versions. Most organizations will choose the appropriate program length for a boot camp based on a variety of factors, with cost often being the most relevant.

A popular option is the twenty-four-hour boot camp. Instead of five days of classes, there are four days. Once again, the boot camp consists of a three-hour session from 9:00 a.m. until 12:00 p.m., an hour-long lunch break, and then another three-hour session from 1:00 p.m. to 4:00 p.m., but this time on Monday through Thursday. Friday is then reserved for a full-length, actual-conditions practice test in the morning. The afternoon can be utilized for conferencing with students and/or parents, as well as providing other services, such as college counseling or test registration workshops.

The minimum viable boot camp is the fifteen-hour version. In this case, students still attend for five consecutive days, but only for three hours each day. In fact, if too many students enroll to accommodate in one class section, running two fifteen-hour boot camps, one in the morning and one after lunch, can be a tenable solution. Since the students will have more time between class sessions and less time in class, assigning homework is more productive than during a twenty-four- or thirty-hour boot camp.

Below is a sample syllabus for a fifteen-hour boot camp and a thirty-hour boot camp. If you decide to run a longer boot camp, such as either the twenty-four- or thirty-hour version, you can reduce the amount of homework assigned by administering some of the sections as practice work during class. One word of caution is that administering entire SAT or ACT sections as practice sets in class can be overwhelming and counterproductive without enough time allotted for reviewing the questions. In fact, students are often better served by breaking up full SAT or ACT sections into ten- to fifteen-minute sets followed by an equal amount of time spent on reviewing challenging questions or questions requested by students.

FIFTEEN-HOUR BOOT CAMP

SESSION	DAY AND TIME	SUBJECT	HOMEWORK
1	Monday 9:00 a.m.–12:00 p.m.	SAT Reading	CB Test 1 and 2, Section 1
2	Tuesday 9:00 a.m.–12:00 p.m.	SAT Math	CB Test 1 and 2, Section 4
3	Wednesday 9:00 a.m.–12:00 p.m.	SAT Writing	CB Test 1 and 2, Section 2
4	Thursday 9:00 a.m.–12:00 p.m.	SAT Essay	CB Test 1 and 2, Section 5
5	Friday 9:00 a.m.–12:00 p.m.	SAT Math	Full-Length Practice Test

THIRTY-HOUR BOOT CAMP

SESSION	DAY AND TIME	SUBJECT	HOMEWORK
1	Monday 9:00 a.m.–12:00 p.m.	SAT Reading	CB Test 1, Section 1
2	Monday 1:00 p.m.–4:00 p.m.	SAT Math	CB Test 1, Section 4
3	Tuesday 9:00 a.m.–12:00 p.m.	SAT Writing	CB Test 1, Section 2
4	Tuesday 1:00 p.m. –4:00 p.m.	SAT Math	CB Test 2, Section 4

5	Wednesday 9:00 a.m.–12:00 p.m.	SAT Essay	CB Test 1, Section 5
6	Wednesday 1:00 p.m.–4:00 p.m.	SAT Math	CB Test 3, Section 4
7	Thursday 9:00 a.m.–12:00 p.m.	SAT Reading	CB Test 2, Section 1
8	Thursday 1:00 p.m.–4:00 p.m.	SAT Math	CB Test 4, Section 4
9	Friday 9:00 a.m.–12:00 p.m.	SAT Essay	
10	Friday 1:00 p.m.–4:00 p.m.	SAT Writing	Full-Length Practice Test

One customization that you can make is to remove the essay instruction in favor of either more reading, math, and writing section practice or some content review. Since the essay is optional, and many colleges have chosen not to include an essay score in their standardized testing requirements, some students have de-emphasized the essay in their preparations. From my conversations with college admissions, I still recommend including essay instruction in most programs, since admissions officers will review SAT and ACT essays, sometimes going so far as to consider them as supplemental writing samples. Completing the SAT or ACT essay can also be a valuable submission from students interested in writing, whether creative or academic.

A weekly class offers many of the same benefits as a boot camp in terms of allowing for longer class sessions to ensure plenty of instructional and practice time but opens up the entire school year for scheduling. Rather than requiring several consecutive days' worth of availability from students, a weekly class can be taught over the weekend or on weekday evenings. Additionally, rather than fitting courses into a holiday week that may occur several weeks before a targeted test date, a weekly course can begin whenever convenient for the staff or students and run on consecutive weeks right up to the targeted test date.

Once again, you have the option of crafting a course that fits your and your students' schedule and availability. I have taught weekly classes of varying lengths at different institutions and in different situations. A thirty-hour course is usually the longest class I teach, which tends to run for ten weeks, with each class session lasting three hours. The shortest class I would recommend would be the fifteen-hour version.

The primary reason I recommend class sessions of three hours in length is that the biggest hurdle to successful student completion of a program is attendance. It is often an easier path to success to expect students to attend ten three-hour sessions than fifteen two-hour sessions or twenty one-and-a-half-hour sessions when building a thirty-hour program. Fewer sessions mean fewer opportunities for students to miss and a shorter period of a student's life during which you are asking for their commitment to your program. You know your student population in a way I cannot, so use your best judgment in building out your schedule and setting up your syllabus.

Whether you choose to hold a holiday week boot camp or a weekly class, please include break time in your class schedule. Most adults have difficulty maintaining focus for more than an hour at a time. Expecting a high school student to do the same is folly. Depending on the student population, holding a three- to five-minute break every hour or every forty-five minutes gives students a chance to use the bathroom without disrupting or missing class, grab a snack, and generally refresh and reset their focus. Some populations require more frequent breaks. Further, breaks not only benefit the students, but they help instructors as well. I can't count how many times a well-timed break gave me a few moments to gather my thoughts or to adapt to an unforeseen circumstance.

When I work with public and charter schools, the best option for these institutions to include the maximum number of students as possible in a program is to hold the course during the school day. This usually takes the form of a once-per-week (required) elective called College Counseling. Schools can choose to offer test prep as an opt-in course, but what I have observed is only the most self-motivated students, or most interested and/or anxious parents, opt into these programs. An opt-out required college counseling elective will not only reach virtually the entire junior class but has the effect of benefiting students who would not ordinarily volunteer to take such a class.

In my year working with schools as a representative of a third-party vendor, such as a tutoring company or nonprofit, I have observed numerous different methodologies employed by schools when setting up such a program. Most schools group students by availability due to their course schedules into several sections that meet with a trained test prep instructor once per week. The class period used for such a course is usually "borrowed" from a study hall period, but I have seen schools take a period from gym class or another noncore course.

A typical schedule would look something like this:

Tuesdays	D-Block	College Counseling (Test Prep)	Ms. Jones

Whether your school employs a rotating schedule or not, or your school's class periods last forty-five minutes, fifty-five minutes, or an hour and a half, you can adapt your instruction to fit in a school day schedule. The most important factor is confirming that your students receive a minimum of fifteen hours of contact with the test prep material in class. This often means that a school day course targeting a spring test date, such as the March SAT date for example, will begin far earlier in the school year than one might expect.

A syllabus for a school day program at a school with forty-five-minute class blocks might look like the following:

TUESDAY COLLEGE COUNSELING CLASS

SESSION	DAY AND TIME	SUBJECT	HOMEWORK
1	September 3	SAT Introduction	
2	September 10	SAT Reading	CB Test 1, Section 1
3	September 17	SAT Reading	
4	September 24	SAT Math	CB Test 1, Section 4
5	October 1	SAT Math	
6	October 8	PSAT Preregistration	
7	October 15	SAT Writing	CB Test 1, Section 2
8	October 22	SAT Writing	

9	October 29	SAT Essay	
10	November 5	SAT Essay	CB Test 1, Section 5
11	November 12	SAT Essay	
12	November 19	SAT Math	CB Test 2, Section 4
13	November 26	SAT Reading	CB Test 2, Section 1
14	December 3	SAT Writing	CB Test 2, Section 2
15	December 10	SAT Essay	CB Test 2, Section 5
16	December 17	PSAT Score Report Return and Review	
17	January 7	SAT Math	CB Test 3, Section 4
18	January 14	SAT Reading	CB Test 3, Section 1
19	January 21	In-Class SAT Registration	
20	January 28	SAT Writing	CB Test 3, Section 2
21	February 4	SAT Essay	CB Test 3, Section 5
22	February 11	SAT Math	CB Test 4, Section 4

23	February 18	SAT Reading	CB Test 4, Section 1
24	February 25	SAT Essay	CB Test 4, Section 5
25	March 3	SAT Writing	CB Test 4, Section 2
26	March 10	Final Review and Wrap-Up	

Obviously, schools across the United States utilize different scheduling mechanics in building out their daily and weekly schedules. Starting from the above as a template, you can create a syllabus that works best for your institution.

As you may have noticed, I have included the homework assignments in the above syllabi. I will explain the homework, what it is and what it means, over the rest of this chapter below.

Lesson Plans

As professional educators know, a lesson plan is a document which outlines what should happen during a teaching experience, usually a daily class period. Since most teachers have completed a course of study that includes learning how to construct and use lesson plans during their undergrad or graduate career, they are equipped to build their own lesson plans for an in-school or school-sponsored test prep program. In my experience, however, many test prep programs are run by home-school collectives and nonprofit organizations like the Boys & Girls Club. The adults running these programs may not have experience constructing and using lesson plans.

I have reproduced a sample lesson plan here, based on the program that I have taught over the last few years since the 2016 redesign of the SAT. It is far less formal and structured than a lesson plan written by a teacher working at a public school would be. The idea is to provide a basic template for a lesson plan so that folks new to teaching can have a place to start but also a jumping off point for experienced teachers to build their own lesson plans.

After teaching SAT and ACT programs for over twenty years, I built my own lesson plans, which I have shared with Livius, the company for which I work, and the tutors who are a part of my team. All of my tutors start with my lesson plans, and as they gain in experience or apply their own experience from years of teaching, they expand on them to suit their own styles and strengths.

The following is part of the first lesson of instruction on the general information on the test and the program. I leave it up to individual teachers to personalize this material, add essential questions or other lesson plan requirements, and adapt as necessary for your environment.

SAT Structure

- Five sections
  - Evidence-based reading and writing (English)
  - Reading
  - Writing and language
  - Math
    - No calculator
    - Calculator
  - Essay (optional)

SAT Scoring

- Two scores
  - Evidence-based reading and writing (English)
  - Math (both sections combined)
- Scale of 200–800
- 1 point for each correct answer
- 0 points for each wrong or omitted answer
- Raw score scaled
- Median score is 500 for each section
- Anything above 500 is "helpful"
- Anything below 500 is "unhelpful"
- Total score of 400–1,600
- PSAT scale is 160–760 per section and 320–1,520 in total
- Use for comparison

Goal Setting

- Identify your previous scores
- Use a previous real PSAT, practice test, or comparison test result
- What are your college goals?
- Select your top choice college or a well-known school that appeals to you
- Find the score range for that college online
- How much are you willing to put into your own improvement?

General Test-Taking Skills

- Guidelines for test preparation

- Dealing with the bubble sheet
- Mark up your test booklet
- Dump the Trash and Mine for Gold

Don't worry if that last test-taking skill is new to you. I will go into detail on both general test-taking techniques and standardized test strategies in upcoming chapters.

As you can see, the lesson plan takes the form of an outline in which you, or the instructor you've hired, can fill in the details and complete specific activities around building, acquiring, or understanding information. I have observed five different instructors, all working for the same tutoring company, all teach a subject as simple and specific as dealing with the bubble sheet in five completely different ways. Especially considering the use of technology and other resources, each instructor can bring something different to the students' experiences.

Given the amount of material in the strategies part of this book, it is essential that you take the time to break down your schedule into lesson plans so you not only know what to accomplish in any particular lesson, but how to accomplish it and how much time you plan to take to do so. The most important aspect is often deciding what examples and sample problems you intend to use and how you intend to explain the concepts. Lesson plans are a map that help you get to where you want to go.

HOMEWORK

There is quite a debate going on in education and parenting circles about the efficacy of homework. The current consensus is that too much homework is counterproductive, especially considering how much a student can expect to learn in a given day. Teachers at progressive schools throughout the country are experimenting with different models and have found that assigning less homework can actually improve student morale. More importantly, current research shows that targeted homework, such as short reading assignments, limited practice sets, and more project-based assignments, can have a bigger impact on learning than traditional homework.

This is especially true for full-year or even semester-long courses at elementary, middle, and even high school levels. Over the years, my own opinion of the amount of homework that should be assigned has moderated. When I first started teaching, I was willing to pile on the homework in the hopes that something, anything, would get through to students.

Now, I tend to think of test prep program homework more like the practice a student needs to complete between music lessons or sports games/matches. Imagine a student who is taking violin lessons. Each week the student meets with the violin teacher. At the end of the semester, the student will participate in the big concert. The violin teacher expects the student to practice the skills and the specific pieces of music for a little bit each day leading up to each lesson and to the concert at the end of the semester.

The same is true of test prep homework. Each week, the student has a lesson or class with the instructor with the goal of taking the SAT or ACT in twelve to fifteen weeks. In between each class or tutoring session, I expect my students to complete a small amount of homework to practice the strategy skills we discussed in the lesson. Luckily, both the SAT and the ACT content is based on material that students should have learned in school over the previous three to five years, so I don't spend a lot of time teaching my students how to read or do basic calculations.

The homework for an SAT or ACT program is, instead, designed to reinforce the test-taking skills that the students is learning. If test prep was only about relearning to read or relearning to calculate, then students would likely not need to do much if any homework. The lessons would be enough. Test-taking skills, however, are not something most students learn in school. What we teach is about critical thinking, problem-solving, and reasoning skills. General content knowledge is essential to maximizing a student's results, but specific content knowledge of a particular passage or word problem is not particularly important. How to break down passages and word problems to find answers is what is important.

SAT and ACT homework should give students the time and practice they need to build test-taking skills. A moderate amount of homework following each test prep session does that. For example, following an SAT reading lesson, I will usually assign a single SAT reading section. Following the very first SAT reading lesson, that assignment is usually section 1 from the Official SAT Practice Test 1. That is a sixty-five-minute assignment that students must accomplish by the next lesson one week later.

More importantly, I do not ask the students to complete the section within the time limit. In fact, I insist that they do not time themselves. I go even further. I recommend that students break up the reading section and complete one passage and its questions per day for five consecutive days. The goal is to master the reading section strategies, regardless of how much time that takes. I know that there will be the opportunity to practice the timing of the test later. Initially, I want the student building their test-taking strategies, which are the key to better results.

Each lesson tends to generate a single section of homework, although I may assign an essay and a writing section during the same week, from time to time. I never assign my students full-length practice tests for homework. In fact, I generally recommend that a class only complete a single full-length practice test as part of a program, as I will describe in detail in the next section of this chapter.

You can find tutoring companies that recommend and administer a full-length practice test every week during a test prep program. Indeed, there are programs that involve no actual instruction, but instead consist solely of students taking a practice test every week for months before an actual SAT or ACT test date. In my opinion, this is insanity.

Imagine a student athlete, such as a high school football player. Every Friday night during the autumn, that student has a game. During the week, does practice time involve a full game every day leading up to the Friday night game? Of course not. Practice involves skill building. Practice involves watching video, studying playbooks, and practicing specific plays and maneuvers. No one would think that playing a full game every day leading up to the actual game is a good idea.

This is the flaw in the "drill and kill" plan of taking a full-length practice test every week leading up to the actual SAT or ACT. While a student who does that may build up a resistance to the emotional stress of the actual test, that student is losing out on diving deep into individual skills represented by specific questions, as well as the opportunity to revisit and review the academic and content-based skills that support those questions.

More importantly, taking a four-hour-long exam every week for weeks on end is demoralizing and dreary. There are diminishing returns on that overwhelming methodology, and I would rather give the student what they need in a more efficient manner while not absorbing all of their time.

Especially at the beginning of a program, all homework should be untimed; however, building endurance is an important aspect of any test prep program. Both the SAT and ACT are three- to four-hour-long tests. Generally, I advise students to spread out a homework section over several days during the first third of a program. In the middle third of a program, I usually introduce the concept of stopwatching.

Stopwatching is when a student completes a homework section all in one sitting but does not strictly time the section. Instead, students should use the stopwatch feature in the clock app on their phones, or an actual stopwatch, to see how long it takes to complete a full section. Often, students surprise themselves by completing sections in far less time than they feared it would take. Even when a student exceeds the time limit, it is a valuable lesson to learn about oneself. Rather than estimate how long they are taking on sections based on their feelings, they now know exactly how long it takes them to complete those sections.

Only in the last third of a program do I assign timed homework sections. Now that students know how long it takes them to complete sections, they can work on adjusting their pacing. Most students begin programs fearing they will run out of time, and rush as a consequence of that fear. The opposite is more commonly true. Most students, especially on the SAT, finish with time to spare, wasting valuable time sitting around after they have answered all of the questions. The pacing they work on while doing timed homework is to train themselves to slow down on those sections.

For sections in which students actually exceeded the time limit during the stopwatch process, especially on ACT homework sections, pacing is just as important. Here, students can decide how they want to spend their time on the sections in which they regularly run out of time. For example, through the ACT science section homework, a student can identify a particular topic or passage type on which they regularly struggle, then plan to work around that topic or passage, spending time on topics and passages that will likely result in more correct answers.

PRACTICE TESTS

The "drill and kill" method of homework tends to overlap with the concept of assigning a practice test toward the end of a test prep program. Since I assign targeted homework assignments based on the content of the specific lessons, students are completing one full section, sometimes two, per week of class. As I explained in the previous section, students build familiarity and comfort with the timing mechanism of the SAT or the ACT by working through a progression from untimed homework sections through stopwatched sections culminating with regularly timed sections.

The point of attempting to complete a homework section within the time limit is not to pressure oneself to finish on time, but instead give oneself permission to slow down in order to fully utilize the strategies from the program on each individual question. I cannot emphasize this enough; students are encouraged by the time limit to rush through the questions out of fear of running out of time. That reduces scores. Slowing down, which I admit seems counterintuitive, maximizes scores by giving students the time they need to fully apply strategies to each question.

While the ACT is designed in a way that makes completing any of the sections within the time limit extremely difficult, it is still important to avoid rushing. Practicing without the time limit (by stopwatching) and then with the time limit can help students understand what they can and cannot accomplish within the time limit. Once students know how much they can get done within the time limit, they can do so without fear of the time limit.

Practicing with timing allows students to build comfort and confidence with the structure of the test. It also builds endurance, since they know how much they need to do and how much they can do in a given amount of time. This leads directly to the practice test. I generally recommend that an SAT or ACT program include a single, full-length practice test as part of the program. As I mentioned previously, multiple, weekly practice tests are not only demoralizing, but can be counterproductive. On the other hand, not taking a full-length practice test is a missed opportunity for students to apply the timing skills they have learned through the untimed-to-stopwatched-to-timed progression of practice on homework assignments.

Schools, tutoring centers, and other organizations tend to hold practice tests during one of two points in a program. Some organizations hold a practice test following the final class or tutoring session, while others do so at a point between the halfway mark and the end of the program. I generally recommend holding a practice test at a point about two-thirds to three-fourths of the way through a program. This way, students will have completed the initial instruction of strategies, had a chance to complete several homework assignments, worked on their timing, and been exposed to most of the content of the program. Additionally, taking a practice test before the end of the program allows for time to be dedicated to reviewing the practice test in class, which can be very helpful to students.

A practice test can be a valuable tool for students to gauge their progress in a test prep program, which is why I recommend that you host one. On the other hand, in and of itself, a practice test is not particularly important. Students learn very little from the experience of taking it, since you are unlikely to be able to accurately replicate the actual conditions on test day. If you are able to use the results of the practice test to enhance the instruction of the final lessons of your program, however, a practice test can be invaluable to crafting a productive and successful program.

POSTPROGRAM FOLLOW-UP

Too often, the relationship between a student or family and the instructor or administrator of a program evaporates once a test prep program ends. The student takes the test, whether SAT or ACT, and then waits to see what result she has earned. The results tend to post approximately three weeks following the test date, initially online, followed by a paper score report that arrives in the mail one or more weeks later. Whether satisfied with the results or not, most students and their families do not follow up with their tutor or instructor to share the results. The exception is in the case of a disappointing result. Especially if the family has paid for tutoring, parents will usually follow up if the result is lower than expected, or worse, lower than a starting score.

When the news is good, though, you, as an instructor or administrator, may never know. Tutoring companies spend a great deal of effort reaching out to families in the weeks following each of the SAT and ACT test dates in the hopes that they hear back from students or families regarding results. While a bad result is never the goal of a test prep program, it is still a result, and can be useful in exploring areas of improvement both for students and instructors. Receiving good news from families is obviously a preferred response, which is why both independent tutors and tutoring companies spend so much time reaching out. Unfortunately, families are not incentivized to share good news.

School administrators don't have this problem. When a student registers for the SAT or the ACT, they enter the name or code of their school during the registration process. Following each test date, the College Board and ACT Inc. send a report to every high school in the country with the results achieved by every student from the school who took the test on that test date. High schools and school districts collect this data and include the results in their reports to the state department of education as a matter of course. In this way, school districts and high schools can identify trends, track program progress, and advise students more accurately during the college application process.

If you are a student, a homeschooling parent, an independent tutor, or a program administrator at a nonprofit organization, for example, you don't have access to these types of reports. Unless you are a homeschooling student or parent, you will likely want to know the results of multiple students, since knowing how your students have done is imperative if you want to know how you have done as a teacher.

One method I have utilized to incentivize students and parents is to offer a prize for sharing the scores with me. I once worked for a tutoring company that offered a ten-dollar iTunes or Amazon gift card to any student who shared their scores with the staff. Approximately 80 percent of the students who took my classes followed up with us shortly after receiving their scores in order to tell us how they did and collect the prize. Of course, the numbers were not enough. The tutoring center director required students or families to either send in a picture of the score report or swing by the tutoring center so we could make a photocopy of the report. Once we had the report in hand, the student received the gift card.

Collecting that data gave us the information necessary to improve our program based on the effect we were having on results. Over time, we were able to adjust how much time we spent on different aspects of the test. We added and removed content-based review, rearranged how much review time we spent on certain strategies, and changed how we assigned practice sets.

If possible, communicate with the students and families after scores are posted. Find out how they did, and you will find out how you did. I realize that offering a prize such as a gift card may be cost prohibitive, but I strongly recommend finding something to incentivize students and families to share their results with you.

Chapter 9
TEST-TAKING FOUNDATIONS

O nce the course or program is created, it is time for instruction to begin. Before we dive directly into the strategies and techniques specific to the SAT or the ACT, let's take a look at tips and skills that can not only have an impact on SAT or ACT results, but academic success in college and beyond. Much of what students learn in a successful test prep program is applicable to learning in general, despite the common misconception that these types of programs only teach skills that can be used on a single type of test that is, ultimately, irrelevant to the rest of a student's life.

Instead, think about a test prep program as stealth instruction for study skills. It is an unfortunate truth that the vast majority of schools have neither the time nor the resources to teach students study skills. Regardless of the value of study skills, schools, their teachers and administrators, are bound by strict budget constraints and laws crafted by legislators with little knowledge of education to stick to a core curriculum of academic subjects. There is no room for nuance or flexibility.

In fact, in many school districts, the only study skills instruction is administered by special education teachers as part of remedial programs designed to help students with learning difficulties. The majority of students, including those in honors and AP programs, don't have access to this instruction, despite the universality of the topics and concepts. This is not meant as a criticism of the fact that students who do receive study skills instruction desperately need it. Instead, I believe that such instruction would benefit every student.

On occasion, students will encounter certain teachers, often English language arts or social studies teachers, who incorporate some study skills instruction into their lesson plans. But this is not the same as a unique program designed to introduce study skills concepts to the student body as a whole. Because of what the SAT and ACT are, however, study skills instruction is a core tenet of a successful program.

GOAL SETTING

All too often, students, as well as parents, educators, and school administrators, fall into the trap of thinking that they are in competition with their peers. While it is true that the college admissions process is technically *competitive*, it is only so in terms of the fact that many colleges can and do turn down applicants. In other words, students may not gain admission to every college to which they apply.

There is another, healthier, way to look at this process, however. Given that there are more than 4,300 colleges and universities in the United States, and just as many, if not more, outside the United States, it is unlikely that two students, even at the same high school, will be applying to exactly the same pool of colleges. Even when students want to apply solely to highly prestigious colleges, such as Ivy League schools, and end up applying to similar colleges from the same pool of schools, they are not really in competition with each other. They are in competition with themselves. Everyone seems to forget that the college admissions process is a singular, personal experience. It is about each student's individual journey from high school to college to the world at large. Every student comes from a different place, has had a different life, and has unique interests and goals.

This means that a successful college application is not about beating other students by achieving higher grades or higher test scores. It is about authentically identifying one's own interests and matching them to one or more colleges that can satisfy the academic, social, extracurricular, and cultural needs of that student.

So, the first step in achieving successful admission to a college that will be the best fit for any particular student is identifying and setting personal goals. Goal setting is the first study skill that I teach in any test prep course. In order to achieve success, a person must know what success means. The simplest way to define success is to establish a goal, and then craft a plan for achieving that goal.

In general, goals should be clear and specific. The more accurately a person can define goals, the more likely that person can achieve them. Saying "I want to get a high score" is not establishing a clear and specific goal. What does a "high score" mean? It can mean anything. "I want to be a doctor" is a far more specific goal. It has meaning, because we all know what a doctor is. That is an example of a long-term goal.

A long-term goal is one that takes a great deal of time and effort to achieve. Within any long-term goal, there are going to be a series of medium-term goals, each made up of numerous short-term goals. A medium-term goal might be "I want to earn an A in Organic Chemistry class." An organic chemistry class is an intense experience, so a person who takes that class will need to set many short-term goals based on individual assignments, quizzes, and exams.

Achieving a useful score on the SAT or ACT is an example of a medium-term goal. It generally takes a few months to achieve such a goal but doing so is not something that students do in isolation. Taking the SAT or ACT is a step in achieving an important long-term goal: earning admission to the best fit college of their choice.

The first goal I ask my students to set for themselves is a score goal. In other words, I ask them what score they would each like to end up with on the SAT or ACT. This answer should be different for each student. I do not want my students to exclaim that they are all shooting for a "perfect" 1,600 or 36. That is a not a goal; it is a fantasy. Yes, there will be students who reach a 1,600 or a 36, but those scores are not necessary for admission to any college or university. There is no college in the world that only accepts students who earn a 1,600 or 36 on these tests.

In order to craft a realistic and achievable score goal, students need two pieces of information. Most students already have one but need to think carefully about the other. The first is a previous result on the SAT or ACT. Most students take either the PSAT or the PreACT in October of their junior year, and many students take these tests in sophomore year as well. Other students begin a test prep program having already taken a preprogram practice test, like those discussed in the previous chapter. This previous result is the starting place for students. It is from this result that the student will want to improve.

The other piece of information is the score range of one college to which the student wants to apply. Some students know exactly what college(s) interest them, while others remain undecided on what colleges they like until the application deadline is looming. Regardless of this, all students should pick a college that they like, even if only a temporary choice, for the purposes of goal setting.

Once a student has selected a college to use for goal setting purposes, they should look at the scores of the students that the college has accepted to see where they should set their goals. Imagine there is a student who has decided that they like the University of Nebraska–Lincoln. According to data submitted to the College Board's BigFuture website by the university, 11,906 applicants were accepted for admission to the school for the freshman class entering in the autumn of 2017, the last year reported. The accepted students had a score range of 22–29 composite on the ACT and 1,130–1,360 total on the SAT. Select a goal based on the range, whether you are looking for entry into consideration by aiming for the bottom of the range, or you are aiming for the middle of the range in order to make your scores a solid part of your application package.

If you would like to review what a score range is, pop back to chapter 5 for a complete explanation. The point of setting a score goal is to establish that each student needs to take the process seriously. Once students know what they need to accomplish in the class, they can work with the instructor to formulate a plan of action. This means achieving a series of short-term goals based on each lesson and homework assignment.

TEST ANXIETY

As a test prep instructor, I often hear parents and students try to rationalize a lower-than-expected previous score on the PSAT or a preprogram practice test. They tell me that the student is a "bad test taker" or something similar. When I ask these students or parents to explain what that means, the answer is usually that these students do well in class and on their homework, but struggle on tests, whether in school or on standardized tests like the SAT. The students and parents insist that the students know the material, and in fact can often articulate or explain everything either verbally or in writing, or both, but struggle to do so on test day.

What I have observed from working with many of these students over the years is that being a "bad test taker" is generally not an innate problem. Most people are not born as a "bad test taker," although students with learning difficulties do find summative tests challenging. For the majority of students, however, being a "bad test taker" is the result of low confidence and poor planning. Therefore, the solution is to build confidence and to learn to create a solid study plan.

Building confidence with the material covered on a test depends on several factors. Communication is the first of these. Often students struggle on test day because they did not prepare for the material facing them. The solution to this is to communicate with the teacher. Find out what, exactly, will be on the test. Obviously, most teachers will not provide the test questions in advance, although a small number of teachers do just that, confident that despite doing so, the test will still provide an academic challenge to students. Rather, students should inquire as to what topics and concepts will be covered by the test. Knowing what is coming is the first step in feeling prepared.

Beyond what concepts are covered on the test, knowing as much as possible about the structure and format of the test is an important factor in feeling prepared for the test. While it makes sense that most students would study in the exact same way regardless of how the questions are asked, that can be counterproductive. There is a great deal of difference between short-answer questions, multiple-choice questions, vocabulary-based questions, and essay questions. Different question types require different methods of preparation. Knowing what students face will always reduce the uncertainty and fear they feel when it is time to take a test.

In order to maximize preparedness, students must construct a specific plan for studying. The average student believes that the only path to success on a test is to study every concept covered in a class since the last test. Again, this is counterproductive. The most efficient plan is to study only what a student doesn't know. In other words, a confident student will refer back to previous homework assignments, quizzes, and tests to find the answers that the student answered incorrectly and use those questions as the launching point for what to study. The confident student trusts that she still knows what she previously knew and answered correctly.

For example, imagine a student taking a world languages class, such as Spanish. This theoretical student earned a 70 percent on each of the last three vocabulary quizzes. When a summative test approaches, a confident student will spend time studying the 30 percent of questions that she answered incorrectly, rather than all of the questions. Not only does this reduce the amount of time spent studying, leaving time to complete other work, but it focuses the student on what she needs to know going forward. Reducing the scope of what needs to be studied usually reduces stress and anxiety. Not only is the student actually more prepared, but the student *feels* more prepared.

This process applies to preparing for the SAT and ACT as well. Since these types of standardized tests are not summative tests covering material that students have learned in a particular class but are instead problem-solving tests referring to material covered in school over the last three to five years, reviewing math, reading, writing, and grammar content is often a waste of time. Instead, students should focus on the things that are actually important on the test: critical thinking, analytical reading, and problem-solving. Additionally, these concepts are often things that are not taught in school. Dedicating time to master these concepts is far more productive than relearning Algebra 1 or basic grammar skills.

A successful test prep program will focus the attention of students on test-taking skills but leave room for targeted content review as needed by students, whether in a private, one-to-one setting or in a classroom environment. Too many test prep companies, public high school programs, and private in-home tutors waste the time of students by drilling on content-based skills. Rather than helping the student, this raises the stress levels of the students by overwhelming them with concepts that may or may not even appear on the tests. These types of programs also ignore more important instruction on test-taking skills.

Once a student has crafted a study plan and scheduled the time necessary to study, the next step is making it happen. Execute the plan. This is not always easy to do, especially by one's self. Ask for help. Take a class, work with a tutor, or build a study group. Thinking about what you need to do is not what studying is. Studying is active. Studying means doing things, not thinking about them. Taking action builds confidence and reduces anxiety, but only action that fulfills a plan.

PROCESS OF ELIMINATION

Perhaps the most basic test-taking skill is understanding the concept of process of elimination when working with multiple-choice answers. At Livius, we call this skill Dumping the Trash and Mining for Gold. Not all multiple-choice answers are constructed the same. In any given set of answer choices, there is only one correct answer. On the SAT, and all of the ACT sections except the math, there are three wrong answers. The wrong answers are often designed to distract students away from the correct answer, but many wrong answers stand out as completely unreasonable choices.

An unreasonable answer often has little to no relationship to the passage or math problem to which the question is referring. These answer choices take strong but unrelated positions. If you can identify them, discount them immediately. In fact, so long as you are taking a multiple-choice test on paper, I recommend that you literally use your pencil to cross off any unreasonable answers.

Distractors are effective at tricking students because they seem reasonable. In fact, distractors often seem like better choices because they are the opposite of unreasonable answer choices. They make sense, even though they don't actually answer the question. Common distractors are answer choices which are facts from a passage. Fact-based errors depend on students feeling satisfaction from identifying a fact from the passage, despite that fact not being the answer to the actual question.

Another common distractor is an answer choice that is a detail when the question is asking for the main idea. The reverse is true as well: a main idea answer when the question is asking for a detail or inference. These types of distractors depend on students recognizing the wrong answer from the passage and feeling relieved that they found a reasonable answer choice at all.

Once you have eliminated one or more obviously wrong answer choices, and literally crossed them off the page, if possible, you can focus your attention on the choices that remain. Correct answers are often not obvious, not strongly worded, and not the most attractive answers. They do all have one feature in common, though: they answer the question.

TIMING

One of the enduring features of standardized tests is that they are timed. Conversely, most schools are moving away from timed tests for academic subjects. Even many states are loosening or removing timing restrictions on yearly tests. The theory is that most things in life are not strictly timed. More and more, adults in the workforce are completing tasks at their own pace, whether they work in agriculture, retail, research, or any of a plethora of other fields. While timing does matter for people who work in emergency services, such as first responders, most people don't work in those fields.

As students have less and less exposure to timed tests, the timing mechanisms on standardized tests become more and more of an obstacle for students. The result is that students tend to rush through timed sections on the SAT and ACT. This leads to mistakes. While it may seem counterintuitive, the solution is to slow down and take the time necessary to reduce mistakes, even at the risk of running out of time.

Imagine a student who rushes through the ACT reading section. This section has one of the most oppressive timing mechanisms of any section on any standardized test. Students are given thirty-five minutes to answer forty questions, which are based on four passages of at least eight hundred to one thousand words in length. The vast majority of students who take the ACT are not able to completely read all four passages and answer all forty questions within the time limit. This leads to students rushing through the passages and rushing through the questions, which is why the average number of questions answered correctly is approximately twenty out of the forty.

What if our imaginary student decided to slow down and carefully work through the passages and carefully answer the questions that she could finish within the time limit? Perhaps she would only be able to read and answer the questions for three of the four passages. That means she would only be attempting thirty questions, but if she answered most, if not all, of those questions correctly, she would earn a much higher score than by rushing through and only answering twenty questions correctly.

Building up confidence with timing is an important factor in any successful study plan. The method that we use at Livius to build timing confidence in our students is a three-step process. Initially, all assignments, whether homework or in-class practice, are untimed. In fact, I advise my students that for any homework assignment that involves working on an actual SAT or ACT practice test section, they should avoid attempting to complete the whole section in one sitting during the first third of any program or class. Instead, break up the section by passage, for reading, writing/English, and science sections, or by difficulty zone in math sections. The goal is to focus on building mastery of the strategies and test-taking skills.

As described in Chapter 8, you should utilize the concept of stopwatching to build comfort and confidence with the timing mechanism. Stopwatching teaches you how long it actually takes to complete a given assignment or section. Once you know that, you can work more effectively with the time limits for each of the different sections, whether on the SAT, the ACT, or any other timed test. Just because a test or test section is timed, that does not mean that going as fast as possible is the best answer. Pace, not speed, is almost always the better consideration.

WORKING WITH THE BUBBLE ANSWER SHEET

Time and again I ask my students if they regularly take multiple-choice tests in school, and the answer is generally the same: no. Most high school students encounter short answer and essay questions on tests in school. The only time they work with multiple-choice questions, and the accompanying bubble answer sheets, is on the annual state tests. While understanding how the bubble sheet works might be helpful on such a test, the fact that those types of tests are almost purely knowledge based means that strategic thinking is far less important than on a test like the SAT or the ACT.

While the directions on both the SAT and the ACT make clear that completely filling in the bubble of the answer you choose is important, that doesn't mean that you need to be perfect. Fill in the bubble, but don't spend too much time on it. I would much rather see my students spend time answering questions than fussing over whether or not they have perfectly filled in bubbles on the answer sheet.

There are some common mistakes that students make regarding the bubble answer sheet. Avoiding these common mistakes can mean maximizing a result. Once again, rushing causes mistakes, so mastering the timing skills we just reviewed is equally important in working with the bubble answer sheet.

Any time a student accidentally fills in two bubbles for a single question, the scoring computer will mark that question as incorrect. This most often happens when a student mistakenly fills in the bubble for one question in the line for the previous question. Always double check the question number on which you are working.

This is also true in the event that a student chooses to skip a question, even temporarily. Should you decide to skip a question, make sure to skip that answer line on the bubble sheet. There is no worse feeling than realizing that you have misbubbled a bunch of answers simply because you forgot to skip a line on the bubble sheet when you chose to skip a question in the section.

Work your way quickly and efficiently through the bubble sheet and try to save a minute or so at the end of the section to review the bubble sheet for that section. Look to see if you have made any mistakes. Look to see if you have double-answered a question. Look to see if you have left any questions blank. Most importantly, make sure the answers that you have bubbled match your answers for each question in the section.

One simple way to double check yourself is to circle the answer choice you have selected in the test booklet for each question as you answer them. When I work with students, either in a class or in private tutoring sessions, I have them answer any sample problems, practice problems, or review problems on the test page. When I assign homework, I have the students mark their answers on the test page. I don't have my students use a bubble sheet for the homework until the last third of the program. This forces students to develop the good habit of marking their answers in the test booklet before they bubble them into the bubble sheet. While this may seem like a waste of time, it is a saver of scores.

GUESSING

Now that the College Board has changed the rules of the SAT to remove the dreaded "guessing penalty" that punished SAT takers for making mistakes, students are well served by developing a guessing strategy that can apply equally to both tests. I never encourage my students to guess randomly. I would much rather my students learn the strategies and test-taking techniques to beat the questions, but from time to time, students will likely need to guess.

On the SAT, a guessing strategy is most useful on the math section, especially when students do not recognize, remember, or understand the math concept that the test writers are utilizing for a particular question. This is equally true on the ACT math section. Luckily, the math sections on both tests have some features that tend to collect the questions that refer to the most challenging, difficult, and high-level concepts toward the end of each math section.

I call the strategy the Guess and Skip strategy. Since there is no penalty for answering a question incorrectly on either the SAT or the ACT, guessing can potentially earn a student a few extra bonus points. This could have a small, but noticeable, positive effect on the final score. Students should use this strategy on any math question on which they know, absolutely know, that they will not be able to answer regardless of how much time they might spend on it. It is counterproductive to spend minutes and minutes on a question on a timed test. Any question that will cause a student to get stuck deserves the Guess and Skip.

The Guess and Skip is less useful on the passage-based sections, such as the SAT reading, ACT reading, SAT writing and language, ACT English, or ACT science. While students may temporarily skip some questions, such as main idea questions, until they have read and answered all of the detail-based questions, the idea is that students should answer every question as they go. Should a student find herself stuck on a particular question in a reading, writing, or science section because two of the answer choices seem too similar, there are other strategies that can help students, all of which will be covered in the next chapter.

On any passage-based sections, a more serious concern is running out of time, especially considering that reading passages may take quite a bit of time, and students earn no points for reading, just for answering questions. Should a student discover that the time for a passage-based section has almost expired, rather than rushing pell-mell through the passage and questions, it is wiser to follow the advice from earlier in this chapter. Slow down. Take the time to correctly answer the questions for the passage that you have already worked through carefully. Then, calmly guess on any unanswered questions in the last sixty seconds of the section.

Remember our imaginary student from our discussion on timing? The student who calmly and carefully answers thirty questions in three passages on the ACT reading section is likely to score better than the student who rushes to answer all forty questions in all four passages. Now, imagine the calm student, who has likely correctly answered most if not all of the thirty questions she carefully attempted, takes the last minute of the section to guess on the last ten questions. Perhaps she picks up one or two, or even three, extra points from guessing. Taking her time has even further benefited her compared to the student who rushed through the section in a quixotic attempt to answer all forty questions, and who on average will correctly answer twenty of them.

PRACTICE MAKES PERMANENT

Most people have heard the axiom that "practice makes perfect"; however, all of my experience and knowledge tell me that there is no such thing as "perfect." The universe just isn't built that way. Yes, it is possible to earn a 1,600 on the SAT or a 36 on the ACT, and some people describe those as "perfect" scores, but from my many conversations with former and current college admissions officers, I know that no college, even an Ivy League school, bases any admissions decisions on whether or not a student scored a "perfect" 1,600 or 36.

Instead, I prefer the axiom popularized by internationally renowned American rugby coach Larry Gelwix in the movie loosely based on the high school rugby team he founded and coached: practice makes permanent. Practice allows us to build our mastery of skills and permanently imbed them in ourselves as positive habits. What you do, you learn. What you do, you are. If you want to achieve positive results, make sure your habits are positive.

If you are hoping to achieve better results on a standardized test, earn admission to the college of your choice, and successfully complete a course of study, do the work. And that includes the work outside of class. Consider the homework from a test prep course as the practice you need to make sure you learn, and eventually embody, the skills permanently.

As I have mentioned before, I am not particularly enamored of busy work. Too much of the homework that students encounter in school is busy work. This is a driving force in the current movement in educational circles to reduce or eliminate homework.

On the other hand, some homework has a useful and specific purpose. Remember the analogies of the athlete or the performing artist. A student who wants to play in the big football game on Friday nights must participate in the daily practices in order to know the plays that the team will hope to accomplish on Friday. A student who wishes to perform in the concert on Saturday night must participate in the daily practices in order to know the music. A student who wants to achieve a successful result on the SAT or ACT on Saturday morning must do the homework in order to practice the strategies and techniques that will help her achieve that success.

Chapter 10
THE STRATEGIES

INTRODUCTION

When I investigate test prep programs at most providers, I notice a similar, flawed, paradigm. Tutoring companies usually build their test prep program around content instruction. To prepare a student for the math section of the SAT or the ACT, these tutoring companies review math skill in algebra and geometry. To prepare a student for the SAT writing or ACT English section, these tutoring companies delve into the minutiae of grammar rules. This approach to test prep completely misses the point of the SAT and the ACT. These tests are not about testing recently learned knowledge, not even the ACT. These tests are not similar to the annual skills tests that students take to demonstrate what they have learned over the past year. The SAT and the ACT are tests designed to show colleges how a student thinks, how a student solves problems, and how a student handles pressure. Strategy, not knowledge, is the key to mastering and overcoming these tests.

As a student progresses through the sections of the SAT or the ACT, a pattern of consistency emerges. Each section of the tests revolves around not only answering questions on a variety of topics but understanding what the test writers are asking you to do. Content knowledge is useful, and sometimes essential, but far more important is the ability to dissect and interpret the questions. Once a student knows what the question is actually asking, she can find the answer in a text or solve for the answer using math, grammar, reading, or science skills.

This section of the book is all about the strategies. Broken down by test section, I will describe each strategy and how to apply it to the SAT and/or the ACT. Rather than write original passages, problems, or questions, I suggest we use what the College Board and ACT Inc. have already created. Both of these organizations have released full-length, official practice tests as both a digital document (PDF) and a paper document. If you do not have access to the paper versions of the document through a school guidance/college counseling department, you can download them from the respective websites.

For the purposes of all example and practice problems, I used the Official PSAT Practice Test #1, originally published by the College Board in 2015, and the official ACT practice test 1874F, originally published in 2018. The College Board published a practice essay passage on their website to which I will refer as well. While I can utilize these documents as practice materials and refer to them in relation to our own, original strategies, I will not reproduce any of these documents due to copyright restrictions. Students, parents, and educators are free to download, print, and photocopy these documents, though, so long as you don't sell copies of the practice tests.

Notice how I do not use the practice tests published in the *Official SAT Study Guide* or the *Official ACT Prep Guide* as example or practice problems. Instead, I recommend saving the eight tests in the SAT book and the five tests in the ACT book for homework assignments and full-length practice tests. While five or eight practice tests may seem like plenty, you may find yourself running out of material more quickly than you realize, so be thoughtful about what you assign your students for homework.

You may also notice that I am not arranging the strategies into coherent or specific lesson plans for you. As I have mentioned in chapter 8, I have created numerous lesson plans based on these strategies for the tutors who work for Livius, the tutoring company where I work. In fact, I have created several different versions of these lesson plans based on our tutoring center needs, school partnerships, and online programs. Given the almost infinite variations on a test prep program, I cannot predict how you will organize your program, especially in light of the options I reviewed in that previous chapter.

Teachers, once you have crafted a schedule, you can build out lesson plans based on the time you have available to spend with students. Just make sure you leave time to work through sample passages and problems. Saying the strategies out loud does not mean the students understand the strategies. Step-by-step instruction followed by application practice is essential to mastering the strategies. If you can't figure out how to build your own lesson plans, you can always ask for help.

From this point forward, I will be addressing the strategies directly to the students. Whether you, the reader, are a student, parent, teacher, guidance or college counselor, nonprofit program manager, or school administrator, the strategies are for the students. Feel free to express them in your own words, using your own examples, or supported by your own experiences in education in general or test prep in specific.

SAT READING STRATEGIES

When I teach an SAT or ACT program, I always begin with the reading section. The reading section is simultaneously the least knowledge-based section of either the SAT or the ACT and the section on which it is easiest to demonstrate the problem-solving techniques necessary for success on standardized tests. It may sound odd to describe a reading section as one that is not knowledge based; however, my point is that the rules of the reading sections dictate that prior knowledge plays no part in a student's ability to answer questions about a particular passage. Regardless of the origins of a reading section passage, the questions that follow are restricted to asking about content in the passage. Since the test writers know that it is likely that students will never have seen that passage before taking the SAT or ACT on that date, they cannot craft questions that require outside knowledge of the passage, the topic, or the author. Everything you need is in the passage, so any knowledge the student already possesses is not applicable to the questions.

Given those factors, the reading passages and their questions are the purest expression of the analytical reading and problem-solving nature of standardized tests. What a student does or does not know has no bearing on how well a student performs on the reading passages and their questions. The ability to break down questions, find answers hidden in a passage, and interpret answer choices is exclusively what it takes to do well on a standardized test reading section.

Due to distinct structural differences between the SAT reading section and the ACT reading section, the reading strategies manifest in very different ways. Keep in mind that there is not one single strategy for these sections, but an interrelated set of strategies that our team has organized into a particular method. The methods used for improving results on the SAT reading section and the ACT reading section are different, even though many of the underlying test-taking skills are the same.

As such, I will begin with the SAT reading section. This is not a slight against the ACT, especially given that the two tests are taken by relatively the same number of high school students each year. Instead, I defer to the SAT reading section because of the applicability of many of the concepts to other parts of the test, as you will see later in this chapter.

The SAT reading strategies are based on understanding several truths about the SAT reading passages and questions. First, the passages in the SAT reading section are unlike the reading assignments students encounter in high school. Whether you as a student are reading a book or short story in English class or an article or textbook in history or science class, the idea is that you will learn something useful and, hopefully, important in the text which deepens your understanding of the material being discussed in class.

The passages on the SAT reading section are, instead, disposable passages. The sole purpose of reading them is to earn points toward the SAT's evidence-based reading and writing (English) score. Students are not expected to learn anything new from the passages, or even remember them once the test has concluded. In short, they are not important in and of themselves.

Second, there is a time limit. Even if the time limit on the SAT is relatively relaxed compared to the time limit on the ACT, it is still a factor. I suspect, given an unlimited amount of time to complete the passages and the questions, that most students could answer most of the questions correctly. Unfortunately, students don't have an unlimited amount of time.

This leads to two ways in which students tend to attempt the passages when they don't know our strategies. Most students attempt to read the passage as quickly as possible, trying to take in as much information as possible, virtually attempting to memorize an eight-hundred-word-long passage in the shortest amount of time possible. This leads to students taking into their brain far more information than they need to answer the questions. Given that there is an average of ten questions per passage, the test writers cannot possibly ask questions about every detail in an eight-hundred-word-long passage. Utilizing this method, students take in a great deal of useless information, which can distract them from the information needed to correctly answer the questions.

Some students try to outsmart the test. They skip the passage entirely and start with the questions and answers, hoping to find answers that are reflected in the passage. The obvious flaw in this method is that the answer choices are not trustworthy. Every question in the SAT reading section has four answer choices, of which only one is correct. That means the other three answer choices are incorrect, but generally not so in ways that are obvious. The trickiness of the wording of the answer choices is a defining factor of the SAT. The difference between a correct answer and an incorrect answer on the SAT reading section often hinges on a single word. Skipping the passage puts a student at a distinct disadvantage when dealing with these tricky questions and their answer choices.

Instead of falling into either of these two traps on the SAT reading section, we recommend using our highly successful method: the Zig Zag Method. Consider for a moment the ancient vaudeville joke,

"How do you eat an elephant?" The answer, of course, is, "One bite at a time!" Given that it is an over-a-century-old joke, I forgive you for not laughing. The point of the joke is that an SAT reading passage is like an elephant in that it can be an overwhelming obstacle for students, although not nearly as lovable. Rather than try to ingest the entire passage at once, especially considering that you don't need to know the entire passage to answer all of the questions about it, you should only bite off what you need for each individual question.

This is made possible by the third fundamental truth about the SAT reading section. Virtually all of the questions include line number references. The questions literally tell readers where to go in the passage to find the answers. Utilizing the Zig Zag Method, you can focus on the specific parts of the passage that contain answers and de-emphasize the parts of the passage that do not contain answers.

Rather than a single strategy, the Zig Zag Method is a suite of strategies that work together to improve your results on the SAT reading section. The key to success using the Zig Zag Method is to trust the process and practice the strategies. Only through repeated practice on actual SAT reading sections can you hope to master the method.

1. Survey

The first step in the Zig Zag Method is the survey. When asked what a survey is, most students stumble over the word until blurting out the answer, "A questionnaire?" Instead, the type of survey we want to do is the other common definition of the word. Think of the survey of the passage as a high-level overview. Before you encounter the questions, it is important to know a little about the passage, which can get you into the right frame of mind for the passage.

Begin by reading the summary at the beginning of the passage. The summary is the short paragraph placed before the start of the first paragraph of the passage. The summary will always contain a minimum of three pieces of information: the name of the author, the name of the passage, and the year the passage was published. Often, though, the summary contains more information than that.

While the author may not be someone who you know, the title and year of publication may be more useful than most people realize. In the science and social studies passages especially, the title often contains hints of the main idea of the passage. This is because hard scientists and social scientists are often trained to refer to their main point in the title of their articles or other publications. The year of publication is also useful information. Since many passages were written in the nineteenth century, when the writing style was quite different from that of today, knowing when a passage was written can help you prepare for archaic language and a more verbose writing style.

If you have had a chance to download it, take a look at the Official PSAT Practice Test #1 from 2015. The first passage in this practice PSAT is an excerpt from the novel *Emma* by Jane Austen, originally published in 1815. While *Emma* is one of the most popular novels in literature, with multiple film and television adaptations, it is likely that most eleventh-grade students are not familiar with the novel. Knowing that it was written in the early 1800s, though, can set you up for success by helping you prepare to deal with English that is not modern and a writing style that is much more descriptive and wordy than in more recently published novels.

Next, read the first sentence of each paragraph. The first sentence of a paragraph is normally the topic sentence. Topic sentences tell you what will be in the paragraph, so even if you don't read the paragraph right now, and therefore don't know the details, you will have a good idea of what, generally, will be in the paragraph.

Last, read the last five lines of the passage. Generally, the last five lines will contain the conclusion or summary of the passage. By reading the first sentence of each paragraph and the last five lines of the passage, you should have a good idea of the general tone, flow, and concept of the passage. By having self-discipline and sticking to the method, you will be able to glean this information in around thirty to sixty seconds.

2. Questions

Once you have completed the survey, you are ready to deal with the questions. Dealing with the questions doesn't mean answering questions, though. First, take a few seconds to identify two types of questions that may require a little extra thought: general questions and paired questions.

General questions are exactly what you think they are. They are questions about the passage as a whole. General questions tend to ask about the main idea of the passage, the author's purpose in writing the passage, or the general concepts or character traits woven throughout the passage. Luckily, the SAT test writers have a habit of placing the general questions first in the set of questions. Most passages have one general question, while some have two, and a few have none. Either way, identify the general questions, mark them in the test booklet, usually by circling the question number, and then skip them for now. You will get back to them later.

Paired questions are a question type relatively new to the SAT, having been introduced to the reading section in the 2016 rewrite of the test. Paired questions are literally two separate questions that are connected by a particular feature. The first question asks a typical detail-based SAT reading question; however, there is no line number reference. The second question provides four sets of line numbers in the answer choices and asks you to determine which set of line numbers provides the evidence to support the correct answer to the first question.

In working with students since the 2016 update to the SAT, I have observed that, initially, students dislike dealing with the paired questions. With experience however, students come to appreciate that the paired questions are essentially a two-for-one special. If you can successfully find where the answer is, by answering the second question in the pair, you can usually successfully answer the first question. At this point, you should merely mark up the page to annotate that these two questions are paired together. In the set of questions that accompanies the excerpt from *Emma* in the Official PSAT Practice Test #1 (2015), questions 3 and 4 are paired together, as are questions 7 and 8. Most SAT reading passages have two sets of paired questions.

Once you have identified and marked the general question(s) and paired questions, you are ready to attempt the first specific question in the set. Read the question carefully. You are looking for what the question is asking you to answer. For example, take a look at question number 2 in the reading section of the Official PSAT Practice Test #1 (2015). What is the single word or phrase that tells you what the question wants? In this case, that word is *summarize*. That clue is what we call the Spy. The Spy is the word, phrase, or group of words that are the core of what the question wants from you. In fact, I can simplify question number 2 into, "Summarize the first two paragraphs." I am merely eliminating the unnecessary words in the question. Remember, it is the wordiness of the questions that makes them seem so difficult.

Now that I know what the question wants, I can go to the passage and read where the line references tell me to read. Notice how I have completely ignored the answer choices. That is essential to proper application of this strategy. Three out of the four answer choices are wrong, and wrong in such a way as to distract you from the correct answer. Don't trust the answer choices; don't give wrong answers your attention.

3. Read

Based on the line number reference in the question, go to the passage and read. For question number 2 in the reading section of the Official PSAT Practice Test #1 (2015), what you read is straightforward. Read the first two paragraph, lines 1–14, so you can summarize them. For most questions, though, the task isn't quite so simple. Often the answer to an SAT question is not found within the line numbers referenced in the question, but instead adjacent to the line numbers. In other words, you will often find the answer you seek just before or after whatever line numbers they tell you to read.

The bad news is that you will need to read more of the passage than you expected based on the given line numbers, but the good news is that you will end up reading more of the passage overall than you realized you were reading, which will set you up for success on the general questions.

Once you have read the part of the passage you needed to read to answer the question, do so. Answer the question, but in your own words. Do not go back to the answer choices, yet. In other words, solve first in the passage before you go to the answer choices.

Let's return to our example of question number 2 in the reading section of the Official PSAT Practice Test #1 (2015). Once you have carefully read lines 1–14, how would you summarize those two paragraphs? Over the years, students have answered that question in a variety of ways. The most common answers I have received from students sound like this: "It's about a girl whose mom has died, but she's generally pretty happy and well off." Now that you have solved the question, preferably in your own words, you can finally deal with those tricky answer choices.

4. Return to the Answers

Since you have already solved first in the passage, you should be returning to the answer choices with an answer already in mind. The key to success here is to trust yourself. Find the answer choice that most closely matches your answer. Don't fall into the trap of massaging the answer you found to make it align with a particularly attractive answer choice. That is the exact point of the test writers creating answer choices that sound similar.

For question number 2 in the reading section of the Official PSAT Practice Test #1 (2015), check each of the four answer choices. Which one most closely matches the summary of the first two paragraphs that you stated in your own words while you were in the passage? While many students can pick out the correct answer at this point, some have trouble due to the traps laid into the wrong answers.

5. Resist

If you have trouble differentiating between two or more answer choices when you return to the answers, don't be too hard on yourself. That is what the test writers planned all along. The answer choices are written in such a way so that many of them sound similar. More insidiously, the test writers regularly use certain tricks to distract you away from the correct answer. Let's examine the four answer choices for question number 2 in the reading section of the Official PSAT Practice Test #1 (2015). We'll go in reverse, since many students never read all four answer choices. Often, when students come across an answer choice they like, they stop and never check any remaining choices. The test writers count on this. By starting with answer choice D, we can break this pattern and force ourselves to check all four. You don't have to do this with every question, but it can be a useful exercise every so often.

Answer choice D states, "A character has a generally comfortable and fulfilling life, but then she must recover from losing her mother." Many students choose this answer choice. In fact, in my experience, this is the most commonly chosen wrong answer. Yes, this is the wrong answer. But, why? What makes this answer choice wrong? Everything in the answer choice is factually true, you might protest. Let's find a way to resist this answer choice. Look for any word or phrase which doesn't work. If even a single word in an answer choice is wrong, the entire answer is wrong. So, look at the way the answer is worded: "A character has a generally comfortable and fulfilling life, but then she must recover from losing her mother." The words *but then* tell us a story of timing. According to the passage, "Her mother had died too long ago for her to have more than an indistinct remembrance of her caresses. . . ." Therefore, the timing in answer choice D is wrong, so the whole answer is wrong. We call this clue the Double Agent, because it betrays the answer choice in which it resides to help you, the student.

Answer choice C states, "Largely as a result of her father's wealth and affection, a character leads a contented life." The Double Agent in this answer choice is subtle; it is the phrase *as a result*. While the passage does mention her father's affection and the fact that Emma is rich, the passage does not state that Emma is happy *because* of her father's affection or her father's wealth.

Answer choice B states, "An affectionate governess helps a character to overcome the loss of her mother, despite the indifference of her father." During my years teaching this lesson to students, my students and I have found three different Double Agents in this answer choice. First, by making the answer about the governess, the answer seems to indicate that the passage is about her and not Emma. Second, the governess doesn't help Emma overcome the loss of her mother, since Emma barely remembers her. Third, her father is not indifferent.

That leaves answer choice A, "Even though a character loses a parent at an early age, she is happily raised in a loving home." Not only are there no Double Agents in this answer choice, but it is the last remaining answer. To quote Sir Arthur Conan Doyle from his Sherlock Holmes stories, "If you eliminate the impossible, whatever remains, however improbable, must be the truth." In other words, by process of elimination, answer choice A must be correct. Many students gloss over answer choice A when working through this question, though. Why, you might wonder? Students tell me they find the answer uninspiring or too bland. But that is often true of the correct answers on the SAT, especially in the reading section. Answer choices that are too interesting, that stand out too much, are placed in the choices to distract students. Answers that are reasonable and bland can hide in plain sight.

6. Repeat

While it may seem that we spent quite a bit of time on question number 2, in reality, it should take you less than a minute to read and interpret the question, read the relevant part of the passage, and find the correct answer. Once you have done so, it is time to move on to the next question. Repeat the process of finding the Spy in the question, reading the passage, returning to the answer choices, and resisting the incorrect answers for each subsequent question.

7. Return for the General Questions

Once you have answered all of the specific questions for a passage, you can return to tackle the general question, or questions, that you previously skipped. For the first passage in the reading section of the Official PSAT Practice Test #1 (2015), that would be question number 1. To attempt this question without having read the passage, except for the survey, would have been difficult. Once you have completed all of the specific questions for that passage, and therefore read most, if not all, of the passage, though, it should be far more reasonable to attempt this question. The Resist strategy is particularly useful for general questions, since it is unlikely you will go back and read any particular part of the passage to answer this question.

Review

I would never recommend to students that they read everything in this way, especially not works of literature. The joy of reading a novel or short story, a play, a nonfiction narrative, or even a textbook, is diving in and losing oneself in the world that the author creates, whether fact or fiction. SAT reading passages are not that. They are disposable passages placed as an obstacle for you as students to overcome in order to earn as many points as possible. For you to achieve that goal, you must practice the Zig Zag Method on every single SAT reading passage. Practice makes permanent.

ADDITIONAL SAT READING STRATEGIES

Within the Zig Zag Method, students can encounter a few types of questions that require a little extra strategic attention. Here, we will discuss strategies specific to particular types of questions. Keep in mind that you should not utilize these strategies instead of the Zig Zag Method, but as part of the Zig Zag Method.

1. Vocabulary in Context

In the 2016 update to the SAT, the College Board removed the last remaining vocabulary puzzles that had been the hallmark of the SAT verbal/critical reading section since its inception in 1926. Your parents probably remember struggling to master analogies and sentence completions while lugging blocks of prepurchased flashcards around in their backpacks back in the 1970s, 1980s, or 1990s. Going back decades, college bound students dedicated an unwieldy number of hours each week during junior and senior year to learning "SAT words." Luckily, those days are firmly in the past.

Vocabulary used to be a major factor in success on the SAT. The last remaining vocabulary questions on the SAT are the handful of vocabulary-in-context questions that accompany each passage. The vocabulary-in-context questions do not require you as students to learn obscure vocabulary last used in everyday English in Abraham Lincoln's day. Instead, they ask students to focus on a concept called multiple-meaning words. A multiple-meaning word is a word which has more than one legitimate meaning. One of the most common examples of a multiple-meaning word is *fire*. *Fire* can mean the hot, burning stuff in which you should never stick your hand. It can mean to relieve someone of employment. It can mean to discharge a weapon. It can mean to start an engine. But it cannot mean all of these things at once.

Let's look at question number 5 in the reading section of the Official PSAT Practice Test #1 (2015). Question 5 asks, "As used in line 26, 'directed' most nearly means. . . ." All four of the answer choices are legitimate definitions of the word *directed*, which is why you should never look to the answer choices to solve the question. Instead, follow the Zig Zag Method. The Spy in the question is easy. What does the word mean "as used in line 26"?

Clearly, reading the word *directed*, or even the entirety of line 26, is not enough to answer this question. We are looking for context. At the minimum, you should read the entire sentence that includes the word in question. Often, you will need to read from the sentence before through the sentence after the one containing the word in question. Context is everything in this type of question. In fact, for this particular question, I advise students to start with the beginning of the sentence on line 19.

"Even before Miss Taylor had ceased to hold the nominal office of governess, the mildness of her temper had hardly allowed her to impose any restraint; and the shadow of authority being now long passed away, they had been living together as friend and friend very mutually attached, and Emma doing just what she liked; highly esteeming Miss Taylor's judgment, but directed chiefly by her own."

    a. trained.
    b. aimed.
    c. guided.
    d. addressed.

In reading the sentence, you should replace the word in question, in this case *directed*, with a simple, common, everyday word of your own choice. In the years I have been teaching this strategy with this passage, students have most often given me responses of *led* or *guided*. At this point, following the Zig Zag Method, students return to the answer choices to find answer choice C matches their own answers most closely. This method works with all vocabulary-in-context questions.

2. Graphics-Based Questions

Relatively new to the SAT, graphics-based questions refer to any charts, tables, graphs, or diagrams which may follow a social studies or science topic passage on the SAT reading section. This structure was added to the SAT as part of the 2016 update in response to critiques of the SAT reading section by educators at both the high school and college level that the test passages and questions did not appropriately reflect the type of reading that students tend to do in college. Specifically, the idea is that you as students are generally faced with academic reading which is often accompanied by data in the form of graphics.

The graphics-based questions ask you to either draw conclusions based on the limited information presented in a graphic or interpret information presented in a graphic in relation to text from the passage. Many students have given me the feedback that they find these questions challenging, since the graphs are often relatively simple and don't seem to provide as much information as they should, based on what the question is asking them to find.

That is the secret to graphics-based questions. The data in the graphic are usually fairly simple, so the strategy is to follow the Zig Zag Method. Break down the question to find what exactly is being asked of you. Then apply that to the graphic, keeping in mind that overthinking the question or the graphic is the trap the question writers have laid for you.

Let's look at question number 18 in the reading section of the Official PSAT Practice Test #1 (2015). This question is part of the second passage, which refers to questions 10–19. After reviewing the summary before the passage during the survey phase of the Zig Zag Method, we can determine that this is a social studies passage, and has something to do with social networks. Question 18 asks us to "summarize" (the Spy) the information in the graph that follows the passage.

Many of the students with whom I have worked look at the graph and begin to spin dramatic tales around what the graph represents. The strategy, though, is to keep it simple. The y axis of the bar graph is the amount of digital information shared in zettabytes, which a note below the graph describes as one trillion bytes, quite a bit more than the gigabytes I can fit on my laptop. The x axis is labeled in years, starting with 2005 on the left and ending with the estimated value for 2015 on the right. A quick glance at the graph tells me that the amount shared consistently rises, as shown by the rising bars moving from left to right. Additionally, the bars start out rising minutely, but the bars grow by increasingly large amounts over time.

Following the Zig Zag Method, I have ignored the answer choices as I worked through the question and read phases. Now I return to the answer choices and attempt to find the answer that most closely matches what I have summarized in my own words. Answer choice A refers to "computers and cell phones" owned by people. Since the graph doesn't mention people, computers, or cell phones, we know that it is incorrect. Answer choice B states the "number of people sharing information has more than tripled since 2005"; however, the graph refers to information and time, not people, so that is incorrect.

That leaves us with answer choices C and D, which both correctly refer to "digital information created" per the graph. Many students end up choosing answer choice D at this point, since it states a fact that according to the graph, the "amount of digital information created and shared is likely to be almost 8 zettabytes in 2015." It is factually true that the graph states that. But that is an example of what I call a fact-based error. While factual, answer choice D doesn't actually answer the question. Instead, answer choice C, "The volume of digital information created and shared has increased tremendously in recent years," best summarizes the graph. The graph overall shows that the volume of digital information has in fact increased in recent years.

3. Paired Questions

I previously mentioned the paired questions in the questions phase of the explanation of the Zig Zag Method. Now, let's look at how to handle this particular challenge. Take a look at question numbers 14 and 15 in the reading section of the Official PSAT Practice Test #1 (2015), also part of the second passage.

Question 14 asks a particularly tricky question: "The author indicates that, in comparison to individuals, traditional organizations have tended to be . . ." Our first task is to find the Spy in the question. What clues or hints tell us what we are looking to solve? The key words and phrases of "in comparison to individuals, traditional organizations . . . (tend) . . ." are what will help us find the answer. But where to look? Question 15 gives us four sets of line numbers. According to the Zig Zag Method, we are now in the read phase. Go back to the passage and read each of the four supplied sets of line numbers searching for a comparison between individuals and organizations. Only lines 66–72, answer choice D, refer to both individuals and large organizations, so we know that we have found *where* our answer is. Now we must delve between the lines to find *what* the answer is.

According to lines 66–72, individuals, empowered by social networks, can take on tasks previously only available to large organizations, and with better efficiency, lower costs, and greater ease. Now we can Return to the Answers in question 14 to see what choice matches the answer we found in the passage. Remember that the question is asking us about the traditional organizations, not the individuals. All four answer choices look relatively similar, another good example of why you should never let the answer choices trick or confuse you until you already know what the answer is. Answer choice D is the only one which describes traditional organizations as less efficient and more expensive, which is in opposition to what the passage says about individuals. Answer choice D is the correct answer to question 14.

One last note about question 14. Notice how the passage described individuals in certain positive terms, but the question and answer twisted that to use the same terms to describe traditional organizations in a negative light. You have to remember that all questions on the SAT reading section are inference questions. They never ask you about the details but about what you can figure out using the details.

4. The Paired Passage

The vast majority of the students with whom I have worked have told me that they have found the paired passage the most difficult part of the SAT reading section, especially before learning about it. The paired passage takes everything challenging about an SAT reading section passage and doubles it. Not only that, the final few questions in a paired passage set are unique in the section because they ask students to compare and contrast two different passages and authors.

The paired passage is one of the social studies or science passages, and is in fact not a single passage, but two 400–450-word passages, written by two separate authors, that share a single set of ten or eleven questions. The paired passages also share something else; they discuss the same concept or topic but have very distinct and different opinions on that concept or topic.

The trick built into the paired passage is that most students, particularly those who have had no guidance on taking the SAT, will tackle the paired passage in such a way as to put them at a clear disadvantage. Most students will read both passages and then start answering the questions. The trouble with this is that the first few questions are about the first passage, but the student has just finished reading the second passage. In other words, the student will have the wrong information available to them at that moment.

The solution is to "supersize" the Zig Zag Method. Apply the method to the *first passage only*. Answer the questions for the *first passage only*. Once that is complete, then handle the *second passage and its questions only*. Not until you have completed all of the questions that refer to either the first or second passage solely should you attempt the compare and contrast questions.

The compare and contrast questions can be considered the most difficult questions on the SAT reading section. Many of the students I have observed struggle with these questions, going to far as to claim that they feel that the College Board is asking them to "mind read" the authors of one or both of the paired passages. Take a look at question number 46 in the reading section of the Official PSAT Practice Test #1 (2015). The question asks how the authors of passage 2 of the paired passage would "most likely respond" to a word used by the author of passage 1.

At first glance, this would indeed seem to ask students to read the mind of authors that they have never met, and in fact have likely just discovered for the first time. This is not the case though. What the question is actually asking is for you to use the information you have gleaned from the passage, specifically the author's main idea or point of view. If you can articulate the point of view of the authors of the second passage, given the hints and clues in the title and text of the passage, then you can ask yourself, "If I held that same opinion, what would I think of the given word in the selected line of passage 1?" That is a much easier question to answer.

Students who follow these applications of the Zig Zag Method to the paired passage can frequently turn a trap into an opportunity for success. In fact, the key to beating the SAT reading section is to slow down and deal with one thing at a time. The whole point of the SAT is that it is an overwhelming experience, so simplification is the best solution to not get overwhelmed.

SAT WRITING AND LANGUAGE AND ACT ENGLISH STRATEGIES

After the 2016 rewrite of the SAT by the College Board, the SAT writing and language section and the ACT English section are more similar than they have ever been. Both sections present a student with several relatively short passages on a variety of topics written at the early high school reading level. These passages are seeded with grammatical errors and other writing flaws, and the students are tasked with identifying whether or not there is an error and which answer choice provides the best solution to fixing the error.

The SAT writing and language section and the ACT English section are often described as multiple-choice grammar sections. Grammar is an important part of the both sections, but much less important than most people realize. The forty-four questions on the SAT writing section are split into two distinct topics, both with their own subscore, as listed on an official SAT score report: *Standard English Conventions* and *Expression of Ideas*. Standard English conventions means grammar, and that accounts for twenty of the forty-four questions on the SAT writing section. The other twenty-four questions come from the expression of ideas topic, and most students, parents, educators, and school administrators are not sure what the College Board means by expression of ideas.

On the ACT English section, there are seventy-five questions, of which only forty fall into the subscore for conventions of standard English, or grammar. The other thirty-five questions are in the two subscore categories of production of writing and knowledge of language, which were formerly combined and called rhetorical skills. Like the expression of ideas subscore on the SAT writing and language section, the rhetorical skills subscores on the ACT represent a confusing and vague set of concepts for most students, parents, educators, and administrators.

That leads to the most common mistake in teaching the SAT writing section: focusing on grammar instruction. The majority of American-born high school students in the United States are much stronger in grammar than they realize. A decade or more of English language arts instruction with a heavy emphasis on writing, combined with facility with spoken English, means that these students have been using relatively proper English grammar for most of their lives. While most students don't necessarily know the names of all of the grammar rules referenced on the SAT writing section, they are familiar enough with the rules that they are not often confounded by the questions or grammar concepts.

Since our program focuses on the strategies for defeating the test as a puzzle, we don't provide a great deal of direct grammar instruction.

Luckily, there is a myriad of tools available in both paper form and on the internet for students, parents, and educators. I recommend delving into grammar instruction only if necessary, based on preprogram practice test results, whether you have chosen to administer a practice test or you use actual PSAT/PreACT results.

Instead, our strategies look at how the College Board and ACT Inc. have structured the SAT writing and language section and ACT English section. We have built our strategies around the types of questions they ask and how they formulate answer choices. While grammar review may be necessary for many students, it is not necessary for all students, and I leave the decision up to you. You know your students (or, if you are a student, yourself), your community, and your current academic situation far better that could I, so you can decide whether or not to include direct grammar review instruction in your individual program. My best piece of advice, though, is to teach the strategies first, then work on grammar as the students complete homework and prove they have mastered the strategies.

1. The Zig Zag Method

The first thing I always point out to students when I teach a lesson on the SAT writing or ACT English sections is the layout of the passages and questions. For an SAT program, I once again utilize the Official PSAT Practice Test #1 (2015) for example passages, beginning with the first passage, entitled "A Nod to Nodding Off." For an ACT program, I frequently utilize the official ACT practice test available to download from the ACT website since autumn of 2018, ACT 1874F, beginning with the first passage, entitled "Mystery Paper Sculptor." Alternately, I utilize one of the sample English passages in the instructional part of *The Official ACT Prep Guide* (2019–20), "The Music of the O'odham," currently on page 221 of the most recent edition of the book.

Grab one of these sample passages and take a look at the page. What do you see? On the left-hand side of the page is a passage, spread out, oddly, over several pages. On the right-hand side of the page are a series of questions. Interestingly, many of the "questions" contain no actual question, but instead, only a list of answer choices. Where is the question? It is the underlined portion of the passage. On both the ACT and the SAT, each question refers to a numbered unlined portion of the passage. This is the question.

The concept is that, if there is an error, whether grammatical or otherwise, it will be found in this underlined portion of the sentence or paragraph. Neither the College Board nor ACT Inc. have a specific name for the parts of the sentence or paragraph which is not underlined, so I call those parts the Anchor, because it anchors the student to reality. If there is something off about a sentence, something that doesn't agree or make sense, it must be the underlined portion, the question, that contains the answer. The Anchor is grammatically correct by definition.

Since the focus of the SAT writing and ACT English sections are on grammar and writing skills, the content of the passages is secondary. As such, students do not need to read the entire passage. That means that a slightly modified version of the Zig Zag Method can be used quite easily to work through each passage. Skip the survey step of the method and move directly on to the read phase for any question which doesn't have an actual question.

As you read the full sentence, not just the underlined portion, ask yourself the same question every time: Is there an error? If not, select answer choice A or F, and move on. The answer to choice A or F is usually NO CHANGE. If there is an error, solve for yourself as to what the error is. Once you know that, you can return to the answer choices and select the answer that solves the problem. If there are two or more answers that seem similar, use the resist part of the Zig Zag Method and eliminate answers that contain Double Agents, the clues that prove the answer choice is wrong. On a grammar section, that clue is usually a new or different error that has been introduced. Then, repeat for each subsequent question.

One side note, you may have noticed that I am referencing both answer choice A and answer choice F. This is due to a particular quirk of the ACT. The ACT uses an unusual system in which the answer choices alternate between A, B, C, and D (and E on the math section) on odd numbered questions and F, G, H, and J (and K on the math section) on even numbered questions. I have never found an answer officially published by ACT Inc. as to why this is done, but I suspect that the answer is that it is an antiguessing tool. Since most students will choose answer choice C when they randomly guess, the alternating letter scheme tends to slow people down and force them to think about the choices more. At least, that is what I have observed.

For questions that contain an actual question, such as number 5 in the first passage of the writing and language section of the Official PSAT Practice Test #1 (2015) or question number 1 in the first passage of ACT 1874F, you can refer to the question phase of the Zig Zag Method to identify the Spy in the question. What is the question asking you to do or find? Keep in mind that any question which contains an actual question is not a simple grammar exercise but is instead an expression of ideas (SAT) or rhetorical skills (ACT) question. I will go into more detail on what these concepts mean in a moment.

One word on the NO CHANGE answer choice first. Many students are very wary of choosing NO CHANGE, and some will never make this choice. The fear that students have expressed to me is that they do not believe that the test writers would ever present a question that does not have an error. This is a strategic mistake. NO CHANGE is one of four equally viable answer choices and will therefore be the correct answer approximately one-quarter of the time. I often caution students that me telling them that NO CHANGE is going to be the correct answer a certain percent of the time is *not* me telling them to count up how often they select answer choice A or F. That way leads to madness. I tell them this to encourage them to trust themselves. Should they come across a question and firmly believe that there is no error, then they should trust that instinct and select NO CHANGE.

Understanding the Grammar Concepts

One last word about grammar. The grammar concepts covered on the SAT writing and language section and the ACT English section are restricted by necessity. There are far too many concepts, many of them quite obscure, for the test writers to include them all on the test. As standardized tests, both the SAT and ACT have a limited number of questions and tend to include the same topics and concepts from testing to testing and year to year.

Both the SAT and the ACT cover three general grammar concepts on the respective writing and language and English sections: punctuation, parts of speech/agreement, and sentence structure. The punctuation questions cover the use of commas, colons, semicolons, and dashes. A short review of colons, semicolons, and dashes is usually sufficient for most students.

Covered under the parts of speech/agreement are concepts such as subject/verb agreement, pronoun/antecedent agreement, number agreement, and other basic grammar concepts. This is the area in which students tend to do best. Most students have an unspoken understanding of these concepts after years of elementary instruction and middle school and high school application.

Sentence structure covers concepts such as run-on sentences and fragments, misplaced modifiers, and independent and dependent clauses. While some of these concepts can be challenging to students, many of them can use their grammar "ear" to hear when something is not structured correctly.

Should you choose to include grammar instruction in your program, focus on these three areas, and avoid delving too deeply into obscure or rare topics. It is a waste of the students' time and can distract them from practicing on mastering the strategies, which is the most important aspect of a test prep program.

2. Expression of Ideas and Rhetorical Skills

Unlike the grammar-based questions, many students struggle to understand what the SAT's expression of ideas and ACT's rhetorical skills questions are asking of them. Often, students can't even articulate what these questions are testing. Expression of ideas and rhetorical skills questions refer to concepts such as passage organization, the flow of information, and the use of language. These concepts go beyond grammar into the style and quality of writing. Even at the high school level, many students struggle to understand, master, or demonstrate facility with these concepts in their own writing. For many students, the expectation that they would be able to identify quality writing or errors of this nature in a passage is faulty. Many students find these nongrammar questions far more difficult than the simpler and more straightforward grammar questions.

The strategy that our team at Livius has developed has had to address not only the concepts that the expression of ideas and rhetorical skills questions utilize in the questions, but the lack of understanding on the part of students in reference to the concepts. Our strategy begins with recognizing what these types of questions are asking students to see, know, and do. On the surface, these questions seem to ask students whether or not they should move, add, remove, combine, or alter the wording of sentences or paragraphs.

The reason students find these questions so challenging is that they have no idea whether or not it is a good idea to move, add, remove, combine, or alter the wording of any particular sentences or paragraphs. For most students, it makes no difference where in a paragraph a sentence is placed. One location is as good as another—except for the fact that that is not true.

Think about the first sentence in a paragraph. What is the purpose of the first sentence in a paragraph? Another way to look at that is to ask yourself, "What is the first sentence of a paragraph normally called?" It is the topic sentence. It is the sentence which tells the reader what the paragraph is about, or what the author is discussing in the paragraph.

Now think about the last sentence in a paragraph. What is the purpose of the last sentence in a paragraph? Or, what can we call the last sentence of a paragraph? In this case, there are two common answers. The last sentence in a paragraph is either the conclusion sentence, wrapping up the point being made in the paragraph, or it is a transition sentence, leading the reader into the next paragraph.

What about the sentences in between? These are the detail sentences. Detail sentences not only provide the evidence or examples to support the topic sentence, but they often do so in a very specific way to help tell the story of the evidence or examples. Even in a nonfiction passage, there is a story that must be told in order for the reader to understand what is happening. Sentences must follow a logical order so that they tell story of the point being made.

Once you understand that each sentence has a particular role to play, or a job that it does, you can then determine whether or not you should move, add, remove, combine, or alter the wording of the sentences or paragraphs in question. If the sentence, part of a sentence, or paragraph is doing its job, then it does not need to be changed. If it is not doing its job, then it is in error, and you can return to the answer choices per the Zig Zag Method to resist the answer choices and find the one that solves the problem. This is why the strategy for the expression of ideas and rhetorical skills question is called the Jobs to Be Done Strategy.

Take a look at question number 5 in the writing and language section of the Official PSAT Practice Test #1 (2015), in the first passage. The question asks us where sentence 3 should be placed in order to make the paragraph most logical. If you had completed the questions numbered 2, 3, and 4, you would likely have already noticed that each sentence in the paragraph is preceded with a number in brackets, such as this: [1]. In fact, if you have completed question number 3, you would have already read sentence 3, but in isolation. This is another reason why students find the expression of ideas and rhetorical skills questions more challenging: they require more reading than the simple grammar questions. To complete question numbers 2, 3, and 4, a student would only need to read the individual sentence to which the answer choices refer. Question 5 requires that students read the entire paragraph.

To successfully answer question number 5, you must ask yourself, What job is sentence 3 doing in this paragraph? Sentence 1 is the topic sentence. It describes a problem. Sentence 2 offers a solution to that problem. Sentence 3 provides evidence for why the problem exists. Sentence 4 supports the solution proposed in sentence 2. Do you notice the problem with the paragraph as it is written? Sentence 3 flows from what is in sentence 1, and sentences 2 and 4 flow together, but are illogically separated by sentence 3. Before we even look at the answer choices, it makes sense that we should move sentence 3 to a spot between sentence 1 and 2. Once you return to the answer choices, you can see that only choice C matches the answer we discovered in the passage.

Utilizing the Jobs to Be Done Strategy you can calmly work through any expression of ideas or rhetorical skills questions on either the SAT or the ACT. The strategy removes the confusion caused by the vagueness of the concepts behind these questions. The strategy does require a great deal of practice, since the ideas behind it are usually very new to most students, but once you master this strategy, the result can be impressive gains in scores and a more efficient pace in the section.

SAT MATH AND ACT MATH

While it is true that there are obvious structural differences between the SAT math and ACT math sections, the math concepts and skills that students will encounter on either test are relatively the same. Both tests cover math topics from middle school through precalculus. The SAT puts more emphasis on algebra and statistics while the ACT puts an approximately equal emphasis on algebra, geometry, and higher-level math. Regardless of which test you take, math skills are useful, but not the most important factor in success on these tests. Critical thinking and analytical reading are essential to success on the SAT and important on the ACT. The secret to success on both the SAT and ACT math sections is strategic thinking.

Rather than a single overarching suite of interrelated strategies, such as the Zig Zag Method on the SAT reading, the ACT English, the SAT writing and language, and the ACT science sections, the math strategies, like the math questions themselves, are independent of each other. Some math strategies are more universal, applying to all, or most, of the math questions on either the SAT or ACT math sections. Many, many strategies fill a much more niche role, applying only to a handful of questions, some of which are quite challenging.

As with any strategies, the key to mastering them is practice. Students must practice the strategies on every SAT or ACT math question. More importantly, instructors must feel absolutely confident in these strategies and should practice them as well, until they become second nature. The more complicated and confusing a math question appears, the more imperative it is that students approach that question from a strategic perspective. Strategies save time and improve results.

1. The Zone Strategy

Unlike any of the passage-based sections on either the SAT or the ACT, the math sections have two distinct features. Generally, each question is independent of each of the other questions. The SAT math section does include a feature where a single concept or graphic is followed by two or three questions that refer back to that graphic or topic, but the questions themselves are not related and one is not necessary to answer another.

More importantly, though, the questions on both the SAT and ACT math sections are laid out in order of difficulty. Order of difficulty means that the very first question in the section is the easiest, and that questions increase in difficulty with each subsequent question number. Ultimately, the final question in the section is the hardest. Accounting for a few blips in the order, the questions start out easy and get harder as you go.

There is one difference between the SAT and ACT regarding order of difficulty. The SAT contains several open-response questions on both the no-calculator and calculator math sections, so keep in mind that the initial order of difficulty for each of the two math sections on the SAT is for the multiple-choice questions only. The small handful of open-response questions, also known as grid-ins, also follow order of difficulty, but considering that there are so few of them, the difficulty ramps up so quickly that most students feel like all of the grid-ins are hard.

Luckily, there is an interesting feature about the multiple-choice questions on both the SAT and ACT math sections. There are exactly fifteen and thirty multiple-choice questions on the no-calculator and calculator SAT math sections, respectively. There are exactly sixty multiple-choice questions on the ACT math section. All of those numbers are divisible by three. As such, it is simple to split the multiple-choice questions into three equally sized zones that roughly equate to where students will find the easy, medium, and hard questions. These are the Green, Yellow, and Red Zones.

Ask any high school student in the process of learning to drive what green means, and they will tell you, "Go! Green means go!" Exactly. In the Green Zone, just go. Don't doubt yourself, don't hesitate, don't second guess yourself. Work quickly and efficiently, and don't let yourself get stuck on any single question. Green Zone questions are meant to be the easiest questions. If a Green Zone question feels difficult, it is likely because you are overthinking the question. Green Zone questions tend to be less tricky, require less math knowledge, and need fewer steps to answer.

The Yellow Zone is based on the concept that a yellow stoplight means "Caution! Slow down!" Yellow Zone questions are more challenging in two ways. They require more math skills and knowledge, and they are trickier and more complicated. This is the zone at which speed becomes a problem. As time ticks on, you'll want to go faster and faster, yet these questions require more time to complete and a more thoughtful approach. Although it may seem counterintuitive, the best way to beat the Yellow Zone questions is to slow down. Avoid rushing and avoid panicking.

Red means stop, but not stop and don't do these questions. Stop and be thoughtful about which questions you plan to attempt and which questions on which you plan to "guess and skip." Except in the case of students striving for an 800 on the SAT math or a 36 on the ACT math, most students should not be attempting all of the Red Zone math questions. Instead, you should be planning to skip questions that are either so confusing as to clearly be timewasters or so mathematically difficult as to be beyond your ability. This does not mean that most students should skip all of the Red Zone questions. There are plenty of questions that are challenging because they are incredibly tricky, but do not contain particularly difficult math concepts. Strategies can help you beat those questions.

There is an additional zone on the SAT: the grid-ins. SAT students should plan to attempt several grid-in questions, especially the first few, which are technically easy questions. Guessing and skipping a few of the hardest, most time-consuming Red Zone questions and instead spending time on several easy to medium grid-ins can result in earning a few extra points, which could translate into better improvement on the SAT. We'll dive into the grid-in strategies later.

Students should practice identifying the zones every math homework assignment, practice test, and in-session review. Knowing where you are in the section can help you manage your pace, build confidence, and reduce anxiety. The Zone Strategy, which I also call the Timing Strategy, is the very first strategy you should learn in an SAT, ACT, or hybrid program.

2. The Reading Strategy

Both the SAT and the ACT contain a large number of word problems, more so on the SAT than the ACT. The toughest obstacle for most students when attempting math problems on the SAT and the ACT is understanding what the questions are asking them to do. Many students try to use their math skills to overcome the problems, when all of the questions on the SAT math section and many of the Yellow and Red Zone questions on the ACT math section are inference questions. If a student doesn't understand what the question is actually asking, math skills alone will not solve the problem.

The key to overcoming math inference questions is a reading strategy. Luckily, the SAT reading section, as well as the SAT writing and language, ACT English, and ACT science sections, utilizes the best reading strategy, the Zig Zag Method. Using the heart of the question phase of the Zig Zag Method, we know that a student must find the Spy in the question in order to understand what the question wants.

The Spy on a math question is twofold. In other words, you should look for two things in each math question: the math Spy and the strategy Spy. The math Spy is the clue or hint that gives away what math concept to which the question refers. This is usually a math vocabulary word. The strategy Spy is the clue or hint that gives away which math strategy you should use to solve the problem.

Take a look at question number 1 in math section 3 of the Official PSAT Practice Test #1 (2015), which reads, "A babysitter earns $8 an hour for babysitting 2 children and an additional $3 tip when both children are put to bed on time. If the babysitter gets the children to bed on time, what expression could be used to determine how much the babysitter earned?" The Zone Strategy tells us this should be the easiest question in this section, so let's not overthink it. The Reading Strategy tells you to read the question, looking for the Spy. What type of math does this question involve? The math vocabulary word in the question is *expression*, so this is likely a pre-algebra question. The answer choices are all sentences, so you don't seem to have to solve anything. In fact, it is likely you only have to apply a little logic to solve this.

Once you read the question, you can refer to the resist phase of the Zig Zag Method and eliminate two wrong answers. The question clearly states that there are exactly two children whom the babysitter will be babysitting, so the number of children is not variable. In fact, it is hard to find a family in the real world in which the number of children a family contains is variable. Consequently, you can eliminate answer choices C and D, where x is the number of children.

Using reading skill and logic, you can see from the question that the babysitter earns eight dollars an hour and can earn an additional three-dollar tip. Given that the three dollars is constant and the total amount depends on a certain number of hours, the best answer appears to be answer choice A.

Despite the fact that this is a number 1, not every student gets the correct answer, mostly due to rushing through the question or feeling overwhelmed by a word problem. The Reading Strategy is based on the idea that a student will work through a word problem actively looking for clues, rather than focusing on the anxiety caused by word problems.

3. Simplify

Any time a student is confronted with an actual equation or calculation problem on the SAT or ACT, this strategy comes into play. Mental math is a powerful skill that schools often begin to teach at the middle school level. Too many students, however, attempt to use mental math in every circumstance, whether or not it is advisable. On the SAT and ACT, for example, the time constraint, emotional pressure, and increasing difficulty level of the math sections preclude mental math much of the time.

Instead, students are gifted with two of the most important tools ever invented: paper and pencil. I always encourage students to write on the math section, taking notes and working through the calculations. While calculators are useful on this test, they are far less useful for solving algebra equations than simple number crunching. Calculators are even less useful for geometry problems. The secret to beating most calculation-based SAT and ACT math problems is to write everything down and work through the steps to a solution. Even in the event that the College Board or ACT Inc. follow through on their plans to administer the SAT or the ACT as computer-based tests starting in the fall of 2020 due to the ongoing coronavirus pandemic crisis, students will be able to use pencil and paper while taking the test on a computer at home.

Take a look at question number 2 in math section 3 of the Official PSAT Practice Test #1 (2015). Before the word problem part of the question even begins, students are presented with a basic algebra equation: $3(x + y) = y$. The question asks for a ratio of x/y, however. Even though this Zone Strategy tells us that a number 2 should be an easy question, many students are stumped by this problem.

Begin by writing down the given equation in your own handwriting. There is something very powerful about writing. Problems that seem impossible printed on the page suddenly make more sense when rewritten in handwriting. Now, simplify. Literally, make the equation simpler. The more complicated and confusing something looks, the more challenging it may feel to make it simpler. The way to do this is to focus on action. Use your math verbs.

Start with what is confusing and complicated about the equation, such as the parentheses. How do you eliminate parentheses in math? Through distribution. Now we have $3x + 3y = y$. Still not simple enough, though. Now, let's balance the equation by subtracting $3y$ from each side of the equation. Now we have $3x = -2y$. Still not simple enough. We can do one more thing, I think. Let's divide both sides by 3, and we get $x = -(2/3)y$. There is nothing more to simplify.

At this point, some students might get stuck. If you find yourself stuck at a point like this, go back to the question. What is the question actually asking you? The question wants the ratio of x/y. All we need to solve this is to know the value of either x or y. And it appears that we just discovered the value of x. Now we can substitute $-(2/3)y$ for x, and we get $-(2/3)y/y$. The last step is to cancel the y/y, because that always equals one, and we are left with $-(2/3)$.

Lo and behold, that is the same as answer choice B, and we have solved the problem. Write everything down and depend on your math verbs: distribute, balance, divide, substitute, cancel, and so forth.

4. Pick a Number Strategy

The first three math strategies, the Zone Strategy, the Reading Strategy, and the Simplify Strategy, are relatively universal. Students will find they use the Reading and Simplify Strategies on most questions, and the Zone Strategy on every question. The remaining strategies are more targeted in their usefulness. When applicable, they are essential. Otherwise, you don't need them. Let's start with the Pick a Number Strategy.

Before you can use this strategy, you must first determine when to use it. The most common example is an algebra word problem in which all four answer choices are expressions with variables rather than real number answers. Take a look at question number 11 in math section 3 of the Official PSAT Practice Test #1 (2015). According to the Zone Strategy, this is a Red Zone question, so it is meant to be challenging. The question is simply worded, however: "Which of the following is equivalent to $(s - t)$ (s/t)?"

We know this is algebra, because of the expression in the question. The first impulse of many students is to try to solve this algebraically, but the expressions are deceptively difficult due to the different structures of the two expressions. Simultaneously, I notice that the answer choices all contain expressions as well, so the Strategy Spy tells me to apply the Pick a Number Strategy.

In this strategy, you will simplify the question by picking one or more small, easy-to-calculate numbers to substitute in place of the variables, in order to solve the problem mathematically rather than algebraically. Let's pick 8 for s and 4 for t. In this case, the question becomes, "What is the value of $(8 - 4)(8/4)$?" Simplified, the answer is 4 x 2 or 8.

Unfortunately, none of the answer choices look like an 8.

A) $s/t - s$
B) $s/t - st$
C) $s^2/t - s$
D) $s^2/t - s/t^2$

Or do they? Once again, substitute 8 for s and 4 for t, this time in the answer choices. Test out all four choices. Once you do so, the only one which works is answer choice C.

So, the rules for applying the Pick a Number Strategy are simple:

1. Pick small, easy-to-use numbers, usually between 3 and 12.
2. Write everything down.
3. Test all four (five on the ACT) answer choices.
4. Avoid picking 0, 1, or 2; these numbers can result in false positives.
5. Consider divisibility; pick numbers that will divide evenly to avoid pesky fractions.
6. For problems that require large numbers, pick numbers that are multiples of 10 or 100.

Rule number 6 is often confusing to students, so consider a question that describes a field in which the length is x meters long. Clearly, that number would not be a small number between 3 and 12. Instead, you must pick a large number, but for the sake of simplicity, you should pick a number that can be easily broken up, such as 300 or 1,000.

5. Down the Middle (Pick an Answer) Strategy

Similar to the Pick a Number Strategy, the Down the Middle (Pick an Answer) Strategy is useful for taking challenging algebra problems and simplifying them to calculation problems. The concept is that certain questions that look very challenging actually ask a simple question that requires a simple answer, which happens to be one of the answer choices. Take a look at question number 5 in math section 3 of the Official PSAT Practice Test #1 (2015).

Regardless of the details of the problem, the actual question is very simple: "How many hard puzzles did Tina solve?" One of the four answer choices must be the answer. That means we can use the answer choices to test and solve the problem.

Before we begin, though, take a moment to glance at the answer choices. You should notice that they are in numerical order from smallest to largest. In fact, if you glance through the entire section, you will see the same pattern. Any time there are real number answer choices, they are generally in numerical order, frequently from smallest to largest like in question numbers 2, 4, 5, 10, and 12, but sometimes largest to smallest, like in question number 6.

Since the answer choices are in numerical order, we can use this to our advantage. Begin by testing answer choice C. You begin with C because it is in the middle, especially on the ACT, where the math section still has five answer choices. By testing the middle choice first, you can not only determine if that is the answer but eliminate other incorrect answers if it is not.

Assume that the answer is 25. Tina would have earned 60 points for each hard puzzle she answered, which means a total of 25 x 60 points, or 1,500 points. Since Tina only solved 50 puzzles in the game, according to the question, that would mean that she solved 25 easy puzzles at 30 points per puzzle for a total of 750 points. However, 1,500 hard points plus 750 easy points is a total of 2,250 points. The question clearly states that Tina earned 1,950 points. Unfortunately, answer choice C provides a number that creates a result that is too large. As such, 25 is too large.

Since 25 is too large a number to provide a correct result, any number that is larger would be even more wrong. That means that we can eliminate answer choice D, 35, without even testing it. By testing answer choice C, we have eliminated two wrong answers. There are still two choices remaining, though.

Now test answer choice B. If B is correct, then you are done. If it is not, you are still done, since that will mean that the answer must be choice A. Either way, you only have to test two of the four original answer choices.

Answer choice B states that Tina solved 15 hard puzzles. That would give her 900 points, since each hard puzzle is worth 60 points. Since Tina only solved 50 puzzles in total, according to the question, that means she solved 35 easy puzzles. At 30 points apiece, she would have earned 1,050 points for the easy puzzles. That would give her a total of 1,950 points, just like the question states. That means answer choice B is the answer.

The only rule of the Down the Middle Strategy questions is to always start with answer choice C. Students may fear that this strategy will mean that they have to plug in all four or five answer choices into the question, but as we have seen, students will almost always only have to plug in one or two of the choices to test the question. If you eliminate all but one of the choices, you can logically assume that the remaining choice is the correct answer. To quote

Sherlock Holmes again, "Once you eliminate the impossible, whatever remains, no matter how improbable, must be the truth."

6. Work Backwards

A simple way to make a math problem more complicated is to provide an answer but ask the student to solve for a variable or constant in the middle of the equation. The elegant solution to this quandary is to work backwards. Let's take a look at a low-level example.

Take a look at question number 14 in math section 3 of the Official PSAT Practice Test #1 (2015), which reads, "For what value of h is 24 = h/10 – 6?" This is an open-response question, and we will review specific strategies for these types of questions later in the chapter, but for now look at how the test writers have constructed the question. In the provided equation, the writers have given us an answer of 24, and placed a variable, h, in the middle of an expression. Normally, order of operations tells us to solve for multiplication, then division, then addition, and then subtraction, but in order to get to the variable in the middle of the equation, we have to work backwards.

First, deal with the subtraction problem. In order to get rid of the –6, we should add 6. The basic rule of algebra is that anything you do to one side of an equation, you must do to the other side as well, so add 6 to 24, which gives us 30. Next, deal with the fraction. Since a fraction is merely division written in another form, all we need to do is multiply by the number on the bottom of the fraction (the denominator if you want to be technical), which is 10. Doing that cancels out the 10 on the bottom of the fraction, leaving just h on that side of the equation. On the other side, we also have to multiply by 10, which means we now have 300. What is left tells us that 300 = h, and can now return to the question, which clearly asks us for the value of h.

7. Logic before Math

There are many questions on the SAT math section, and a few on the ACT math section, which require no calculations whatsoever. These math problems rely on logic to solve. Take a look at question number 8 in math section 3 of the Official PSAT Practice Test #1 (2015). The test writers provide an equation, which initially may lead a student to think that calculating is required to solve it, but look at the answer choices. They are all sentences. That is a decisive clue that this problem will likely not involve any actual math.

The question tells the story of a coffee shop and selling a certain number of cups of hot chocolate. The equation models the number of cups sold, n, and the average daily temperature, T, such that $n = 456 - 3T$. The actual question part of the question asks, "What is the meaning of the 3 in the equation?" In other words, the question is not asking you to solve anything, but to understand how equations are constructed.

In technical terms, the number 3 is called a coefficient, which means that it is number multiplied by a variable. In this question, the math terminology is unimportant. What is important is that this is a word problem, and it tells a story. Since T represents the temperature on a given day, on average, you should ask yourself, logically, what would happen when I enter two different values for T into this equation? Keep in mind that I am not asking anyone to solve for those numbers, but instead to think about what would happen. If the temperature was 50 degrees, for example, $3T$ would be 150. Subtract that number from 456, and you would get a result around 300. If the temperature was 30 degrees instead, $3T$ would be 120. Subtracting that result from 456 would get you a much higher value for n, the number of cups of hot chocolate sold.

As we can see, the lower the value of T, the more cups of hot chocolate are sold, which makes logical sense. As the temperature drops, and the value of $3T$ lessens three times as quickly, the number of cups represented by n will go up since we are subtracting a smaller and smaller number from 456. Looking at the answer choices recreated below, logic dictates that means that answer choice D is the only answer that fits.

A) For every increase of 3°F, one more cup of hot chocolate will be sold.

B) For every decrease of 3°F, one more cup of hot chocolate will be sold.

C) For every increase of 1°F, three more cups of hot chocolate will be sold.

D) For every decrease of 1°F, three more cups of hot chocolate will be sold.

Look for ways to apply logic to word problems on both the SAT and the ACT. The longer the word problem and the less math you actually need to do, the more likely you'll need to apply logic. Additionally, questions that include answer choices in the form of sentences or fully constructed equations are often logic questions. Ultimately, any question that never asks you to calculate anything is a logic question.

8. Know Your Math

Since the SAT and ACT math sections are nominally math tests, some degree of knowledge regarding math is necessary. It is very difficult to achieve a useful score without some mastery of math. That doesn't mean that only high-performing math students can do well on the SAT or ACT math sections, but it does mean that every student should have a level of comfort with math skills across a wide variety of topical areas.

On both the SAT and ACT, the majority of the skills come from the areas covered in algebra classes, from middle school through the beginning of high school. The SAT currently includes a large number of questions from middle school statistics, while the ACT includes a swath of early high school geometry concepts.

Build some time into any program to brush up on the skills that your students (you, if you are the student) need to review. The temptation for many teachers is to focus on math skills in the math portion of an SAT or ACT program, which is a common mistake. Going too far and ignoring skill review can be just as harmful to students' improvement.

My advice to the tutors I hire and train is to teach strategies first and then use the second half of a program to review math concepts that have shown up as problem areas. Too often, teachers and tutors want to cover every math concept that might appear on any SAT or ACT math section, but that is frequently a waste of time. Students don't need to study or review things that they have already mastered. Brush up on the topics on which they have identifiable struggles.

Grid-Ins

Unique to the SAT, the student-generated response questions, also known as grid-ins, cause an outsized amount of stress on students. When asked, many students cannot articulate why they fear the grid-ins. By digging deeper, I have realized that uncertainty is likely the root cause of the anxiety that students experience. Since the majority of the questions on the math section, in addition to all of the questions on the reading and writing sections, are multiple-choice, students tend to develop a level of comfort with the multiple-choice format and the multiple-choice answers.

Open-response questions, by definition, do not provide preselected multiple-choice answers. The comfort provided by the multiple-choice answers is absent. This happens regardless of whether or not a student knows how to solve a particular problem. Students have a safety valve of guessing one of the answers on a multiple-choice question. That does not exist in the grid-ins.

The first step in building confidence with the grid-ins is helping the students confront this emotional experience. When I teach an SAT class or work one-on-one with a student in a tutoring setting, I always ask the students to think about the math class they are currently taking, or have recently completed if we are working together over the summer. Whether a student attends public school or private school; is taking Algebra 1, geometry, Algebra 2, precalculus, or calculus; or is working at the college-prep, honors, or AP level, the majority, if not all, of their homework, quizzes, and tests are open-response questions. Very few students respond that their work in school involves any multiple-choice answers at all.

Once students realize this, they can reframe their experience with the grid-ins. Rather than seeing them as something radically different than the multiple-choice questions, they can instead view them as a slightly different format, but one with which they have had years of experience. More importantly, the level of their work in school is most likely far higher than what they will encounter on the SAT. While the SAT includes math topics on the math sections that range from middle school math through the very beginning of precalculus, the vast majority of questions on the test refer to topics that are below grade level for most students. Remember, the SAT applies difficulty to the math sections with confusing word problems, not advanced math concepts.

Keep in mind that the grid-ins also follow order of difficulty, although the test writers are not as strict about that here. There are only five grid-ins in the short/no-calculator section and only eight in the long/calculator section. As such, the difficulty tends to increase more quickly than most students expect.

There are a handful of rules about the grid-ins that students should keep in mind. Understanding how the grid-ins work is one of the best ways to avoid mistakes, reduce anxiety, and build confidence.

- Grid-ins can never have negative answers. Look at the grid; there is no place to bubble in a negative sign. All grid-in answers must be positive or zero.
- Use the answer boxes. While you only get credit for what you bubble into the grid, writing your answers in the answer boxes reduces silly mistakes. You can line up your bubbles to make sure you grid in what you intended.
- Pick a side. If you ever look at the grid-in directions on an actual PSAT or SAT, you will see that you can grid in your answers either justified to the left of the grid or to the right of the grid. Which side you choose doesn't matter. Just pick a side and be consistent with yourself.
- Reduce fractions. Technically, you are not required to reduce fractions to get credit on the SAT. However, some concepts in math, such as ratios and probability, require you to reduce to lowest terms. To avoid silly mistakes, always reduce your fractions to lowest terms.

- Don't round decimals. When you grid in a decimal, use as many boxes as the decimal needs. In other words, if your answer is a long or repeating decimal, you can only round to make it fit in the grid. If you calculate an answer of .6666666666 on your calculator, four boxes will be .666. The computer will therefore read an answer of .66 as incorrect, since it will interpret that as sixty-six hundredths.

- Don't grid in zeroes before decimals. Since you will need to use all of the boxes for your answer, gridding in something like 0.66 would be seen as incorrect by the grading computer. I realize that many teachers in schools require you to write the zero in front of the decimal to get credit for correct answers in school, on homework, and on tests. My advice to students is do what your teachers require in their classes; do what I say on the SAT.

- There are no mixed numbers allowed on the SAT, only improper fractions. Apparently, the College Board's grading computers cannot understand mixed numbers.

- Grid-ins can have more than one correct answer. On occasion, a grid-in question can result in more than a single correct answer. Perhaps the question is a quadratic, which often has two solutions. Perhaps the answer is a range of values. When this happens, choose one of the possible answers, and fill in the bubbles for that sole answer. Don't try to input multiple answers. That does not work.

When students learn and follow these basic rules of the grid-ins, they tend to have a less stressful experience dealing with them. For students scoring in the middle of the possible range of scores, or even lower, the grid-ins can be treated almost like bonus points, especially in light of the Zone Strategy. A low- or middle-range student should focus on the Green and Yellow Zones to pick up as many raw points as possible. Rather than getting stuck in the Red Zone, however, these types of students should attempt the first few grid-ins to grab some extra points.

Guessing

There is always a bit of controversy around guessing on standardized tests. On the SAT in particular, there has been a powerful reason not to guess for many years. From 1940 to 2016, the College Board calculated a "guessing penalty" into the raw score by assessing a quarter of a point penalty for each wrong answer. This was done to discourage random guessing, which was apparently a serious concern in the 1930s.

The ACT has never had a guessing penalty, so guessing was always a viable strategy on that test. The SAT dropped the guessing penalty in 2016, once again proving that the two tests are more similar now than ever before.

My advice on guessing is to do it sparingly. I would rather that my students know how to solve the overwhelming majority of questions, understand the majority of concepts on the test, and are prepared for what they will encounter in each section. Regardless of how much a student prepares, however, the test writers will manage to surprise students on a regular basis, especially on some of the most difficult questions.

One major trap on both the SAT and the ACT is getting stuck for a long time struggling with a single question. Rather than getting stuck, I would rather see a student follow the guessing strategy introduced in chapter 9: Guess and Skip. Even if a student plans to come back to a question once they have reached the end of the section, there is no guarantee that there will be enough time left. I advise my students to enter a potentially temporary answer in the bubble grid in case they don't have the time to come back. If they do run out of time, which is definitely a concern on the ACT, for example, they will have at least answered all of the questions.

Other than on the grid-ins on the SAT, which have no multiple-choice answers, students should never leave any question blank. Even picking up one extra raw point via the Guess and Skip Strategy can be a net positive.

Calculator Use

Especially in light of what students learn in precalculus and calculus, students have a tendency to overuse their calculators on the SAT and ACT. The concepts are so advanced in those classes, and most questions require the graphing capabilities of the most technologically superior devices, that students become dependent on them.

The concepts on the SAT and the ACT, however, range from middle school math to the very barest hint of precalculus. The majority of questions that students encounter on these tests refer to concepts that students learned in middle school and ninth grade. According to documentation published by the College Board, a calculator is not required to answer any of the questions on the SAT, and the ACT writers are almost as adamant about the math on the ACT.

While I tend to disagree with the College Board on a whole host of issues, this is one area in which I am in complete agreement with both them and ACT Inc. When I work with students, I encourage them to work pencil to paper to solve the math questions. A calculator cannot solve math concepts, as it can only do what it is told. In other words, if a student doesn't know how to solve a particular question on the SAT or ACT, the calculator is not going to do it for them.

It is a useful tool, so I do want my students to have one handy on the test, but like any good tool, you should only use it when necessary. I don't use a hammer to unscrew a lightbulb, brush my teeth, or clean my computer screen. I only use it when necessary. I treat calculators the same way.

ACT SCIENCE

To the consternation of many students who love science, the ACT science section is not a test of science knowledge or ability. While exposure to science can be helpful, especially when dealing with technical terminology and obscure concepts, it is not essential to success on this section. It is reasonable for people to believe that the ACT science section requires highly developed science knowledge, especially considering that this was true when the section was first designed by the ACT test writers several decades ago. Surprisingly, though, the ACT science section took on the role of a reasoning and logic section over thirty years ago.

The ACT test writers cannot predict what science classes any given student has completed, especially considering the wide variety of curricula utilized by local and state school districts throughout the United States. Since the ACT test writers don't know if a particular student has completed a high school physics class, it would be patently unfair to base a general knowledge test score on a topic that many students may not have learned in school.

Instead, the current iteration of the ACT science section uses science concepts and terminology to devise reasoning-based puzzles to test students' ability to identify and infer information. In fact, the science section is the only part of the ACT that focuses on making inferences instead of identifying details.

While it is technically true that the ACT science section covers four main topical areas in the realm of science—biology, chemistry, physics, and earth/space sciences—that is far less important than it would be if the passages and questions required specific science knowledge to discover correct answers. Instead, students are better advised to treat the science passages like they do the grammar passages on the SAT writing and language and the ACT English sections.

Rather than worry about the content of the passages, focus instead on the context provided within the passages. Since students are not asked about science knowledge, but merely about the data involved in specific "experiments," they can use test-taking techniques and strategies to identify answers and beat the questions. The first step to doing that is recognizing the structure and format of the passages and adapting accordingly.

According to *The Official ACT Prep Guide*, there are three distinct passage formats used on the ACT science section. This information can currently be found on page 279 of the 2019–20 edition of the book. The three formats are data representation (data rep) passages, research summaries passages, and conflicting viewpoints passages. Once we explore each type of passage, it should be clear why this is far more important for success on the ACT science section than actual science content.

Since *The Official ACT Prep Guide* has the clearest examples of these passage types, I utilize them as teaching examples. In that way, I can save the science sections in all five practice tests in the official book, as well as the science sections in the downloadable practice tests, for homework and full-length, actual-conditions practice tests. As with all ACT sections, timing is a serious concern for students, since they only have thirty-five minutes to complete forty questions, or at least as many as they can do in that limited amount of time. Practicing the science section strategies helps students develop confidence and build up their efficiency in this section.

The sample data rep passage can be found on page 280 of *The Official ACT Prep Guide*. As you can see from the sample passage, a data rep passage is almost entirely made up of charts, tables, graphs, figures, or diagrams. The "passage" part of the passage is a single, relatively short paragraph. According to the ACT, the concept behind the data rep passage is that a student or scientist has completed an experiment and the passage contains the raw data collected. The questions tend to involve identifying details hidden in the graphics, drawing conclusions based on the data, and making connections between different aspects of the data. Interestingly, a deep understanding of the science covered in the passage is absolutely unnecessary. Either two or three of the six ACT science passages will be data rep passages.

The sample research summary passage can be found on page 285 of *The Official ACT Prep Guide*. At first glance, it may look similar to a data rep passage, but a few things will stand out that clearly separate them. There is a good deal more text in a research summary passage. In fact, over the page, there will likely be a balance between text and graphics. Further, the concept behind the research summary is different. The idea is that a student or scientist has conducted an experiment and the passage represents the summary of that experiment, including one or more distinct experiments as well as references to the hypothesis being tested. The questions revolve around making inferences based on the hypothesis and drawing conclusions based on the data. Questions for this passage type likely focus on why the student or scientist did what he or she chose to do. Either two or three of the six ACT science passages will be data rep passages.

The sample conflicting viewpoints passage can be found on page 289 of *The Official ACT Prep Guide*. This passage stands out. With a single glance, you can clearly see that a conflicting viewpoints passage is almost entirely text. In fact, many of them will be. Often, conflicting viewpoints passages contain no graphics whatsoever. The concept behind a conflicting viewpoints passage is that two, three, or four students or scientists have studied a scientific theory or concept and have each come to a different conclusion. In other words, their viewpoints conflict. The questions revolve around interpreting the theory or concept from the point of view of one or more of the students or scientists and comparing and contrasting their different ideas. For multiple reasons—more text, a more complicated passage concept—students tend to find the conflicting viewpoints passages significantly more difficult than either of the other two passage types. Luckily, only one of the six ACT science passages will be a conflicting viewpoints passage.

Due to the balance between text and graphics, most of my ACT students have told me that they found the data rep passages the quickest and easiest of the three passage types. Understanding the timing for each can help students determine if they need to utilize a strategy of skipping the conflicting viewpoints passage in its entirety in order to save it for last, providing they have time remaining at the end of the section. If not, a Guess and Skip strategy is more productive on the conflicting viewpoints passage than any other.

For all three passage types, logic and deductive reasoning are the two primary skills needed for success, especially since actual science knowledge is relatively unimportant. What really matters is the ability to break down the questions, and then quickly find the information in the graphics or text. The following strategies, similar to the pared-down version of the Zig Zag Method utilized on the SAT writing and language and ACT English sections, are the best way to build the logic, reasoning, and problem-solving skills necessary to improve results on the ACT science section. Remember, you don't need to know much about science to do well on this section. Don't let yourself get caught up in technical terms, and don't worry if you don't know how to pronounce these terms.

1. Survey

Any good detective needs to take a first look at a crime scene before attempting to solve the crime. The same thing is true for a successful student on the ACT science section. Take a moment to look over the passage. First, determine the passage type. Next, look over each individual graphic and each specific paragraph. A useful survey should take no more than thirty to forty-five seconds but will give you all that you need to know how to proceed on the passage.

2. Trigger Phrasing

A trigger phrase is a short, one-to-two-word note that the student should write next to each individual graphic or passage. It is a message meant for the student to find when answering the questions moments later. Whether it is a summary of the main point of the paragraph, or a hint to the concept covered in a graphic or paragraph, or a clue to what is contained in the passage in that particular place, a trigger phrase can be a signpost that leads a student from the question to the answer. Writing down the trigger phrases may add ten to fifteen seconds to the survey.

3. Identify the Spy

Students should spend the majority of their time in each passage on the questions. That doesn't mean that students should spend a great deal of time on any one question. As quickly and efficiently as possible, students should break down questions into the words or phrases that tell the student where to look in the passage and what to look for in order to find the answers. As you look at real ACT science questions, you will notice that they are incredibly wordy, oftentimes obtuse. Not every word matters. What is the question really asking you to find? Look for the verb(s), or action word(s), in the question. Then identify any technical terms. Those are your clues. That is the Spy.

4. Mark Up the Data Source

Now that you know where to look in the passage, use the clues in the Spy to find the answer. Unlike the rest of the ACT, the answers to ACT science questions are not generally on the surface. ACT science questions require you to dig into the data source, whether that is a graphic or a paragraph. Mark up the page. Write on the test booklet. If you, or your student(s), are taking the ACT after September 2020, and are therefore taking the test on a computer, take notes on the provided scratch paper. Use the two best tools ever invented in human history, pencil and paper, and figure out what the clues are telling you to find in the passage. Don't think; do.

Review

The ACT science section appears to be a test of science knowledge but is instead a test of reasoning and logic. If you treat it like what it is, you can use the appropriate skills to break apart the questions and then find the answers carefully hidden just below the surface of the passages.

While science knowledge can give a student the confidence not to get tripped up or stuck on the science terms, neither knowing nor understanding those terms usually helps in these passages. Because the test writers cannot guarantee that any individual student will have taken any particular science class before encountering the ACT science section, the science content is merely a structure on which the questions and answers are draped.

ACT READING

At first glance, the SAT reading and ACT reading sections look similar. There is a passage, followed by questions. It is at this point that the philosophical differences between the writers of the SAT and the writers of the ACT become most stark. The two sections could not be more different, and therefore require wildly different strategies to overcome them and achieve useful results.

As previously discussed, the SAT reading section is all about inferences. Every question on the section is an inference question. Since knowing where to find the answers is not nearly enough, the SAT writers are happy to tell you exactly where to look in the passage. For most students, the first obstacle is figuring out what the questions are even asking of them.

The ACT reading section is very different. The passages, while of the approximate same length as SAT reading passages, tend to be slightly easier to read. The questions are detail-based and are therefore more straightforward and easier to understand. The answers tend to be on the surface of the passage, providing you know where to look in the passage.

As such, there are some significant structural differences between the SAT reading and ACT reading sections. On the SAT, the questions follow the order of the line numbers of the passage, and in fact, most of them include line numbers in the text of the question itself. This is not true on the ACT reading section. The questions are in no particular order, and rarely include line numbers in the text of the questions.

So, though the passage and questions may be easier to read and understand on the ACT reading section, the difficulty of the section is just as high as, if not higher than, the SAT reading section, since students have no quick or easy way to find where answers might be in the passage. Couple this with the reduced amount of time available to students during each individual passage, and it is clear why many students consider the ACT reading section one of the most difficult tasks on either test.

Due to the structural differences between the two reading sections, it quickly becomes obvious that the Zig Zag Method is not a viable strategy for the ACT reading section. As such, our team at Livius developed an incredibly useful strategy set around the specific structure and format of the ACT reading section. Once again, it is not necessary to know everything in the passages. The ACT reading passages are also disposable passages, containing far more information than the test writers can access for questions. Like the SAT reading section, the biggest mistake that students can make is attempting to memorize or learn everything in the passage before confronting the questions.

The strategies for the ACT reading section are based on the idea that the questions will tell the student exactly what they need to find, but never where to find it. The goal of the strategies is therefore to help students find information as quickly and efficiently as possible. When one wants to find information about the world around them, there is one perfect tool that can help—a map.

Imagine you are taking a journey from Chicago to Los Angeles. There are many ways to get from one city to the other. You could fly, but you would miss any details of the path between them. You could drive, and see the details, but which route you take will change what you see. If you really want to know what life is like in the small towns and rural areas between those two amazing cities, you would likely want to take the scenic route. Parts of the remaining actual highway, in fact, have been designated a National Scenic Byway.

The Route 66 Strategy helps students quickly create a map of the passage, which they can then access to find the location of answers. As I previously mentioned, the ACT reading section questions concern themselves with identifying and working with details, most of which can be found on the surface of the passage. In fact, students can literally point to the answers in the text of the passage in most cases.

The Route 66 Strategy has two main parts, working with the passage and working with the questions. Since the strategies that revolve around working with the questions are somewhat similar to those on the SAT reading, SAT writing and language, ACT English, and ACT science sections, I will begin with the passage-based strategies.

1. Survey

As always with a passage-based assignment, begin with a short, quick glance at the passage. Read the summary placed before the passage begins to identify the author, the title, and date of publication of the passage, as well as any other provided information. Read the first sentence of each paragraph, and finish by reading the last five lines of the passage. Once again, this presents the student with the topic sentence of each paragraph and the conclusion of the passage. This will provide the student with a powerful glimpse into the main thrust of the passage, what it is about and what the author intended, and the author's tone and style.

During the survey, which should take between thirty and forty-five seconds, make sure to use your pencil to mark up the passage, by underlining or circling. Mark up any key words or phrases that stand out to you, such as proper nouns, numbers (including dates), technical terms or advanced vocabulary words, or anything the author is telling you is important by printing words in bold or italics, or highlighted by underline, in parentheses, in quotes, or separated by dashes. Do not underline or circle the entire first sentence or each sentence in the final five. That doesn't make anything stand out. Choose wisely, but quickly.

2. Rapid Reading

Technically, you've read the passage once already during the survey. Since you only read the first sentence of each paragraph, as well as the last five lines of the passage, another pass through the text is necessary. The mistake that many students make at this point is thinking that a rapid read means reading for details, but a little more quickly than usual. This is not that. The rapid read means reading as insanely fast as possible. The point is not to pick up any of the details, learn anything, or memorize anything. The point is to leave signposts for yourself so that you know where to look when you get to the questions.

As you move through the passage as quickly as possible, mark up individual words or phrases in the text by underlining or circling. Once again, don't highlight everything. Mark up a few words here and there, especially proper nouns, numbers (including dates), technical terms or advanced vocabulary words, or anything the author is telling you is important by printing words in bold or italics, or highlighted by underline, in parentheses, in quotes, or separated by dashes. Then, jot down your trigger phrases.

3. Trigger Phrasing

Just as in the ACT science section, identifying where a piece of information resides is more important than what that information is. Once again, jotting down a one-to-two-word note for yourself, this time in the margin next to each paragraph you complete during the rapid read, is invaluable when you are working with the questions. Don't overthink the trigger phrases. They are not meant to be poetry. Just a word or two about the paragraph, or something that stood out, or an important detail from the paragraph. The most important aspect of trigger phrases is actually writing them down. Don't waste time convincing yourself that you will remember where things are in the passage.

4. Mapping

The good news is that you have been doing this step the whole time. Mapping is the act of underlining or circling words or phrases that stand out in each paragraph. In both the survey step and the rapid read step, the act of marking up the page is mapping. Mapping happens simultaneously with those two steps. It may add a few extra seconds to the first two steps, but it will save you a great deal of time once you start working on the questions.

Midstrategy Review

The Route 66 Strategy is a difficult one to master because it is so antithetical to how people read normally. Once again, there is a vast difference between reading an article in a magazine, newspaper, or online, or reading a novel or short story, or reading an assigned selection from a textbook, and reading a passage on the ACT. At the very least, the timing is different. You are not expected to learn from an ACT passage, just mine it for correct answers.

The whole process of taking Route 66 through the passage should take no more than three to four minutes, leaving students around five minutes to work through the ten questions. That may not seem like a lot of time but remember that the ACT questions are more straightforward than SAT reading questions. They take less time to break down, and once students know where to look in the passage, the answers are easier to find.

Speaking of the questions, let's look at the four strategies specific to breaking down ACT reading questions.

1. Identify (and Skip) the General Questions (for Now)

Specific questions, those that ask about a specific detail or concept within the passage, are much more common than general questions, which ask about main ideas or the author's voice or methods. Take a few seconds before diving into the questions to see if there are any general questions in the set of ten. There may not always be general questions, but it is wise to answer them last, after you have worked through all of the specific questions and had a chance to revisit the passage text numerous times. Only then will you know enough about the passage to safely answer general questions.

2. Identify the Spy in the Question

Each question includes hints as to what it is asking. These key words or phrases tell the student what the question wants to know, and, on the

ACT, where to look in the passage to find the answers. Several words in every question will be redundant or unhelpful, such as a phrase like, "According the passage . . ." Obviously, the answer will be found in the passage. No need to think about things like that.

Once you know what the question wants and where to look, find the answer in the passage. Ignore the answer choices until you find the answer in the passage. Remember, you will almost certainly be able to literally point your finger at the answer in the text. This is how the ACT works.

3. Return to the Answers

Once you know what the answer is, you can return to the answer choices to find it. Attempt to match what you found with one of the answer choices. For most questions, the answer choices will be different enough that you should be able to do this.

4. Identify the Double Agent

Unfortunately, not every question or answer choice is as straightforward and clear as the rest. When you come across a particularly obtuse or wordy ACT reading question or answer choice, don't panic. Luckily, the ACT test writers have a few habits in how they construct the answers. Some sets of ACT reading answers follow a peculiar pattern in which two contain a similar word or phrase, and the remaining two contain an opposite similar word or phrase. When this happens, you will likely want to look for a clue within each answer choice that proves that choice incorrect. This clue or hint is called the Double Agent, since it betrays its own answer choice to help you. Wrong answers always have a Double Agent, and correct answers never do.

Final Review

Take a look at the sample ACT reading questions on pages 257–66 of *The Official ACT Prep Guide*, 2019–20 edition. The questions refer either to a passage about Eleanor Roosevelt, which can be found on page 272 of *The Official ACT Prep Guide*, or to a passage on rural fires, which can be found on page 275 of *The Official ACT Prep Guide*. Use these passages to practice the Route 66 Strategy, and then you can assign full reading sections from the ACT book for homework and additional practice.

The Route 66 Strategy has a steep learning curve, but the benefits are clear. Students who practice the strategy until it becomes second nature on the ACT work at a more efficient pace, answer more questions correctly than when they started, and build confidence in their own abilities.

SAT ESSAY

The SAT essay underwent a massive redesign culminating in the launch of the 2016 version of the SAT. This change was due to the nature of the previous version of the essay. In short, it was too easy. Numerous tutoring companies, including our own, figured out a system for crafting writing that perfectly met the criteria of the rubric for that essay. In other words, we all found a way to game the essay.

Over time, both university admissions officers and the College Board realized this. As such, not only did the College Board design an essay assignment that eliminated the flaws in the previous version of the essay assignment, but the test writers created what I consider to be one of the most difficult and challenging writing samples on a standardized test.

The SAT essay presents students with a passage of approximately one thousand words, which is either an article written by a journalist or columnist and published within the last five to ten years in a real newspaper, magazine, or news website, or an excerpt from a speech or document created by a "great thinker" within the Great Global Conversation, written between the 1790s and the dawn of the twenty-first century. The task of the student is to write a response that analyzes the persuasiveness of the passage in three areas: the author's use of evidence, the author's use of reasoning, and the author's use of stylistic elements.

The problem with this assignment is that very few students have any experience writing this type of essay in school. Students are far more comfortable with writing persuasive responses than analyzing them. In fact, many of the students I have encountered are not even sure what it means to analyze a text.

In simplest terms, to analyze means to answer the question of why. Analysis is the exploration of why something is the way it is. Analysis explores why someone did what they did and how they did it. Unfortunately, most students spend their time on the SAT essay describing what the author said or wrote. In other words, they end up summarizing the passage instead of analyzing the passage.

Clearly, there is a strategy for writing a successful SAT essay, which I will describe momentarily; however, the absolute best piece of advice you or I can give any student before beginning work on the SAT essay section is, "Don't summarize; analyze!" Any student who writes a laundry list of things the author wrote is going to see a lower score as a result. The students who take the time to analyze why the author said or wrote what she did are going to be rewarded with a positive result.

SAT Essay Scoring

One of the reasons why the SAT essay has become so controversial in the last few years is the major change in the scoring system. The old SAT (and the current ACT essay) used a simple scoring range of 1 to 6, with 6 being the highest score. Two people, usually high school English teachers from around the country, read and graded the essay on a simple rubric, and the College Board added the two scores together. The final, combined score was on a scale of 2 to 12, with 12 representing the best score and 7 representing the median score.

The current SAT essay does not have a single score. It generates three separate scores. Students receive a score in three areas: reading, analysis, and writing. The reading score represents how well the graders felt the student understood the content of the passage. The writing score represents the quality of the student's writing, including organization, the flow of the argument, and the avoidance of errors in grammar, punctuation, and capitalization. The analysis score represents fulfillment of the assignment: analyzing the persuasiveness of the author's argument.

Each of the three separate scores is on a range of 1–4, with 4 representing the highest score. As always, there are two graders, and the College Board adds the two scores together. In each of the three areas, a student can earn a score on a scale of 2–8, with 8 representing the highest score possible, and 5 representing the median score. A typical result can look like this:

Reading: 7
Analysis: 5
Writing: 6

One mistake that many students, parents, and educators make is adding the three results together. Neither the College Board nor college admissions officers do that. The example above would appear on the student's SAT score report as a result of 7/5/6, not a combined total of 18.

Since the SAT essay is optional, I usually advise families that if a student can achieve a result of all 5s or higher in the three areas, that student can refrain from taking the essay when signing up to take the SAT a second or third time. The essay is very challenging and stressful, and not taking it can make the experience of taking a subsequent testing of the SAT less painful.

The First Ten Minutes

Before you can begin writing your essay, you must first deal with the passage. Luckily, the essay is a fifty-minute assignment, and despite the fact that the College Board provides four lined pages in which to write the essay, most students will only need to write two-plus pages to achieve a useful score. Since doing that will not require the entire fifty minutes, you can afford to take the first ten minutes to work with the passage.

The first thing you should do is read the passage. Unfortunately, there is no shortcut, no trick, no workaround. You must actually read the passage. More importantly, you should take notes in the margins while you read the passage. This is not something that you are reading for fun. The point is to be ready to write about this passage.

The notes that you take are in direct relation to the assignment. Before the passage begins, you will find a box at the top of the page. Take a look at sample passage 2 on page 173 of *The Official SAT Study Guide 2020 Edition*. Before the passage by Adam B. Summers begins, you will find a box which asks you to consider Summers's use of evidence, reasoning, and stylistic elements. While you read the passage, you should note examples of the author's use of evidence, reasoning, and stylistic elements, and jot down any notes on how or why the author uses them.

My advice to my students is to find a minimum of three examples of each. It is unlikely that a student will be able to explore nine different specific details from the passage in a two-plus-page essay, but it is better to have more examples than you need than too few when you begin writing.

Once you have found your examples, you should take a few moments to plan out what you are going to write about. It doesn't matter if you create an outline, or a mind map, or your own favorite graphic organizer. Just plan ahead.

The trouble many students have at this point is not understanding what the College Board means by reasoning. Most students understand what evidence is, or at least they think they do. Many students know what style elements are. Very few students can articulate what reasoning is.

Reasoning is the argument that the author is making and how it is constructed. What is the author's point, and what are the minipoints that the author makes along the way to build up to the final summation of the point in the last sentence of the last paragraph? This is a difficult concept for students to grasp, and when I teach an SAT class, I spend a great deal of time working through the two sample passages provided by the College Board. In addition to the aforementioned passage by Summers, you can also find sample passage 1 on page 157 of *The Official SAT Study Guide 2020 Edition.*

Once you have collected at least three examples each of the author's use of evidence, reasoning, and stylistic elements, and mapped out a plan for the structure of the essay, you can begin to write your essay. You should have at least forty minutes remaining to write the essay, including a few minutes for last looks.

The Thesis Paragraph

A successful essay must begin with a clear and concise thesis paragraph. This is often a challenge for students. Many students have told me that they dislike writing because they find it difficult to get started. The largest part of that difficulty is crafting a thesis statement. It is often a struggle to codify the point of a passage in a single phrase or sentence.

Luckily, this is not an issue in the SAT essay assignment. The point of the essay is to analyze the persuasiveness of the author's argument. The students' thesis statement should state whether or not the author is successful in being persuasive. All you need to do is to copy down the author's thesis statement and include it in your own thesis. Happily, the College Board literally tells you what the author's thesis statement is.

Take a look at the box which follows the passage in sample passage 2 on page 174 of *The Official SAT Study Guide 2020 Edition*. The task given to students is to write "an essay in which you explain how Adam B. Summers builds an argument to persuade his audience that plastic shopping bags should not be banned." Once again, the College Board test writers literally tell you what Summers's thesis statement is in the task box.

Since the SAT essay is part of a standardized test, and the task is the same every single time, even though the passage is different, your thesis statement will tend to look the same every time. Begin by telling the graders the name of the author, the title of the passage, and the year and source of publication. Next, provide a little context for the grader as to the topic that Summers is discussing over one to two sentences. End with the thesis statement in which you state whether or not the author has been successful in making his or her argument. For example, here is a thesis paragraph for an essay that I could write on the Summers passage.

> In 2013, Adam B. Summers published an article in the San Diego Union-Tribune entitled "Bag Ban Bad for Freedom and Environment." In this article, Summers discusses a law proposed by the California State Senate which would ban the use of plastic bags at large stores throughout that state. The bill was proposed as a measure to protect the environment. Summers is not as persuasive as he would wish in arguing that plastic shopping bags should not be banned.

It may seem strange to students to repeat the name of the author and the title of the article when it is likely that the essay graders will see dozens, if not hundreds, of essays responding to the same passage. But that is actually the point. After a while, all of the essays will begin to blend together for the graders. As a wise professor of mine once said, "Never be afraid to be obvious!" Remind the graders what the passage is and that you know who wrote it.

The Detail Paragraphs

Once the thesis paragraph is complete, students should choose at least one example each of the author's use of evidence, reasoning, and stylistic elements to analyze. Each example should be given its own paragraph, or two, so that students avoid the trap of writing one single, giant paragraph for the entire essay. There is no quicker path to a low score than writing a single, unrelenting block of text.

For each example, you can begin by referring to the text in the passage, but don't fall for the trap of stopping there. Remember, don't summarize—analyze! Once you remind the grader where in the passage your example lives, explore why the author wrote or said what he or she said, how it was used in the passage, and, most importantly, whether or not it is persuasive.

Don't discuss two different examples in the same paragraph, unless you can draw a correlation between them. Give each example its own paragraph to give yourself the space to fully explore the why and how of it. Even if you choose two different examples of reasoning or evidence, give them each their own paragraph.

It has been my observation that more short paragraphs will result in a better score than fewer long paragraphs. Not only are short paragraphs easier to write, but they are easier to read. The easier it is to read an essay, the more likely the graders will reward the student with a higher score.

The Conclusion

If you look at the sample student essays provided by the College Board on pages 159–72 and pages 175–87 in *The Official SAT Study Guide 2020 Edition*, you may notice that not all of the high-scoring sample essays include effective conclusion paragraphs. This likely means that a strong conclusion paragraph is not essential to a high score on this assignment. Most students, however, do not feel comfortable ending their essay without an attempt at a conclusion.

The main trap inherent in writing a conclusion for this type of essay is the temptation to include an opinion on the topic that the author is discussing. Resist this temptation. The task in the second box which follows the passage clearly states that the essay "should not explain whether you agree with" the author or not but focus instead on analyzing the persuasiveness of the author's argument. A successful conclusion refers back to the students' own thesis and ties in the examples discussed in the essay. In other words, restate whether or not the author was successful in persuading an audience, not whether or not you agree with the author.

ACT WRITING TEST

While the ACT writing test assignment also underwent changes in 2016, they were less drastic than those seen on the SAT essay. Not only did less change about the assignment, but the task remains comparatively easy in relation to the current SAT essay. Students are presented with a paragraph about a current event issue, followed by three provided perspectives on that issue. The task is to write an essay that explains the student's own opinion on the issue, along with supporting evidence, as well as analyzes the relationship between the student's opinion and one or more of the provided perspectives.

In other words, students must not only have an opinion on the issue but support that opinion with evidence. Then, students have to write about one or more of the perspectives, both in terms of whether or not they agree with the perspective and why the perspective is correct or not. What should become clear is that this is a hybrid essay, part persuasive opinion piece, part analytical essay.

Once again, since this is part of a standardized test, and the task is the same for every essay even as the content students discuss changes, the format of what students write should tend to look similar for every attempt. The test is standardized, so the written response tends to be standardized. Our strategy involves a repeatable format and structure into which students can plug the details based on the current event issue and perspectives provided by the ACT test writers.

The Prompt

Take a look at the sample prompt on page 302 of *The Official ACT Prep Guide*, 2019–20 edition. The prompt is entitled "Free Music," and the layout on the page is virtually identical to what students will encounter on a real ACT writing test. The "passage" is simply a single paragraph which describes an issue which may be familiar to students. It should take no more than a minute to read the paragraph carefully.

Before moving on to the perspectives, you should take a moment to write down your opinion on the issue. It is imperative that you have an opinion. It is impossible to write an essay defending one's opinion if one does not have an opinion. It is likely that many students will either not care about the issue or have no prior knowledge of it. Regardless of any particular student's experience with the issue, if students find they don't have any opinion on the issue, they should make one up. No one is going to hold you to this opinion. We all know it's just for the essay.

You should then read the perspectives one at a time, taking a moment to jot down two notes on each. First, note the perspective's position on the issue. Generally, one of the perspectives will be in favor of the issue, one will be opposed to the issue, and one will try to find the middle ground between the two extremes. Second, note your own agreement or disagreement with the perspective. Part of the task of the essay is to respond to the perspectives.

Finish up by sketching out an outline or mind map of what you plan to cover in your own essay. Keep in mind that I will explain our strategies for each paragraph of your essay over the next few pages.

The process of working with the prompt should take no more than five minutes, giving you up to thirty-five minutes to write and double-check what you've written. Once again, students are provided with four lined pages on which to write the essay, but most students only need two-plus pages to write a successful, high-scoring essay.

The task, at the bottom of the prompt page, is always the same. The test writers ask that students write a "unified, coherent essay," which basically means treat the response as a single writing assignment instead of writing separate responses to each of the three perspectives. Once you know what you want to write, you should dive right in.

The Thesis Paragraph

As always, you should begin any writing assignment with a clear and specific thesis paragraph, culminating in a precise thesis statement. A good thesis paragraph introduces the concept that you will discuss, so this is the only place in which you should spend any time summarizing the text. The thesis statement should be clearly stated, which means that you will need to literally spell out your opinion on the issue.

Many students fall into the habit of listing the examples they will be exploring in the detail paragraphs, but this is an unsophisticated style of constructing a thesis paragraph, so I discourage my own students from doing this. Instead, describe the concept of the issue, define any terms that might need explanation, and finish with the thesis statement. This will guide the grader into the flow of the argument based on the thesis statement.

The Second Paragraph

Take a look at the sample prompt on page 302 of *The Official ACT Prep Guide*, 2019–20 edition, again. If you look in the essay task part at the bottom of the page, there is a list of goals for this essay provided by the test writers. The second goal is to "develop and support your ideas with reasoning and examples."

This means that the test writers want students to write about a specific example that explains why they hold the opinion expressed in the thesis statement. Most students fail to do this, however. The majority of essays that students produce in their first attempt at writing an ACT essay skip past this from the thesis paragraph directly into a discussion about one of the perspectives. Students forget to develop and support their own perspective first.

The simplest way to do this is to tell a story about why you hold the opinion you hold. Consider the free music prompt. The paragraph explains the concept of free music as meaning streaming music, which often eliminates the need to purchase music, possibly affecting how much people appreciate music. If I were to write about this issue, and my opinion were that streaming music increased my appreciation of music, I would then write a second paragraph telling the story of my experience with the streaming service I use and the new music discovery playlist I receive every Friday.

The Third and Fourth Paragraphs

Over the next two or more paragraphs, you should write about two of the perspectives. I recommend to my students that they choose the perspective with which they most agree and the perspective with which they most disagree. For each perspective explain what it is stating and why you agree or disagree with it. The why is the most important part. In fact, explore that why as far as you can go. Why is the perspective correct or incorrect? What is the perspective not considering?

Not only should each of the two perspectives you discuss get their own paragraph, but don't be afraid to write smaller, shorter paragraphs, rather than single, large paragraphs. It is often easier for the graders to read multiple short paragraphs than it is to read longer paragraphs.

Additionally, be as specific as possible. Add in stories about your experiences with the issue, including observations you've made of your friends and family members dealing with the issue, things you have read or studied in school, watched on television, or seen on the internet. Details provide context and help readers understand the points you want to make.

The Conclusion

A conclusion paragraph is essential for an essay partially based on your opinion. Unlike the SAT essay task, a conclusion to the ACT essay is necessary because you are expressing your own opinion. It is important to return to that to remind the grader what you were hoping to achieve. Restate and rephrase your thesis statement, and then tie together your examples and analyses to show that you have proved the point you intended to make with your thesis.

Chapter 11
CONCLUSION

Now that you have a plan for setting up a program, knowledge about tutoring and how tutoring companies operate, and the strategies for building skills on the SAT and the ACT, you are ready to build and execute your program. Whether you are a student, a parent, a teacher, a guidance/college counselor, or an administrator (whether with a school district or a nonprofit organization), you are now armed with the knowledge you need to prepare yourself and others on how to achieve success on the SAT and the ACT.

This book is a useful tool for designing, building, and administering a program, but don't be afraid to admit that you don't know everything. Even if you now have the strategies to teach an SAT math lesson, for example, you may not be a math teacher, and may not be comfortable with the content of the test. The best advice I can give anyone beginning an SAT or ACT program is simple: ask for help.

Asking for help is not a sign of weakness, but is instead a sign of strength. It takes emotional and mental strength to acknowledge one's own weak spots. Fear of looking foolish or dumb or unqualified is a powerful obstacle, and confronting that fear to ask for help anyway shows true strength.

Whether you reach out to a fellow student, a parent, a teacher, a counselor, or another responsible adult, there is someone out there who wants to help you. In fact, nothing makes a teacher or counselor happier than helping others.

Lastly, we at Livius are here for you. We offer a variety of free and paid programs for students (both online and in-center), for schools, and for nonprofit organizations. You can always just reach out to ask a question of our team or visit our website (livius.me) for more information.

Thank you for reading this book, and let's all keep learning.

INDEX